Also By Barbara Techel

NONFICTION

Through Frankie's Eyes: One woman's journey to her authentic self, and the dog on wheels who lead the way

CHILDREN'S BOOKS

Frankie the Walk 'N Roll Dog
Frankie the Walk 'N Roll Therapy Dog Visits Libby's House

WISDOM FOUND
IN THE PAUSE
Joie's Gift

Barbara Techel

Joyful Paw Prints Press, LLC
ELKHART LAKE, WISCONSIN

Copyright ©2017 by Barbara Techel

Published in the United States by Joyful Paw Prints Press, LLC, Elkhart Lake, WI, www.joyfulpaws.com

Library of Congress Cataloging-in-Publication Data: 2016953089

Editor: Dana Micheli, writersinthesky.com
Cover design: Caryn Newton, lanternglowdesign.com
Back cover author photo: Lisa A. Lehmann, lehmannphotoart.com

ISBN 978-0-9882499-3-6

To Joie. For helping me see the true purpose of life.

When I look into the eyes of an animal I don't see an animal.
I see a living being. I see a friend. I see a soul.

— A.D. WILLIAMS

Contents

Introduction

Coming to a crossroads in life isn't always easy. In fact, it can be downright terrifying. We worry about making a mistake or taking a wrong turn, and because we're uncomfortable with this feeling, we just forge ahead—even when we aren't sure where we are headed. We feel this is what we are *supposed* to be doing. We certainly don't sit still long enough to really listen to what our hearts may be trying to convey to us.

The universe, or as I often call it, Spirit, has its own unique timing. Sometimes we are meant to be forging ahead and at other times we are meant to be resting and reflecting so that the still small voice within can guide us to the next step.

I came to this realization thanks to a pint-sized dachshund named Joie. She taught me the gift of learning to pause, even though I wasn't open to receiving it at the time. To this day, it can still be challenging, but I have come to think of these times of tuning into a deeper awareness as a practice. As for my beloved Joie, she passed away on August 22, 2013. At first I hesitated to share this so early in the book, but ultimately decided it was important for you to know. You see, Joie gave me many gifts, but her greatest gift is when she left her physical body.

While Joie's death was quite unexpected and very painful, it's her profound effect on me that I carry with me today. I often felt her presence while I struggled to write this book, with the push and pull of many feelings vying for my attention and me trying to make sense of them all. Throughout it all Joie was there, quietly nudging me to continue. It was as if she was saying, "Trust the process."

Now I see that this process, which began in November of 2013, included a much-needed pause, although at the time it felt more like a frustrating delay. Finally, I realized I had to set the book aside and try to trust that it would find its way out into the world when the time was right.

That time came on the morning of January 4, 2015. I was lying in bed when suddenly the unfinished manuscript began to tickle my mind. My thoughts began firing at a rapid pace, and no matter how I tried to quiet them, they wouldn't let me go back to sleep. They were beckoning me back to the page, and although I was scared to start again for fear of not finishing, I found them impossible to resist.

With dear, sweet, Joie guiding me from the other side, I now share with you how she came to be in my life. And how her leaving this earth, although way too soon, was all part of a divine purpose. It was a gift that ultimately helped me find my way back to my sense of self once again.

Part One

Joie

CHAPTER ONE

Expanding My Heart

If someone had told me years ago that my first dachshund Frankie would become paralyzed at the age of six, I wouldn't have believed them. And if that person then told me I'd someday purposely seek out and adopt another paralyzed dachshund, I would have truly thought they were crazy.

I remember vividly the day Frankie was diagnosed with Intervertebral Disc Disease (IVDD). She had experienced a fall that left her unable to use her back legs, and I was hoping and praying the damage wasn't permanent. As the vet delivered the devastating news, I was overwhelmed with sadness for Frankie and the feeling that my life would never be the same. Little did I know that we were both about to embark on an amazing journey. That story I tell in my first memoir, *Through Frankie's Eyes: One woman's journey to her authentic self, and the dog on wheels who led the way.*

As I watched Frankie forge on with exuberance and determination despite having to use a wheelchair, I became very passionate about finding a way in which I could share a positive message—the message that even dogs—and humans—with disabilities can lead fulfilling lives.

This led me to write two children's books about Frankie. The same year my first book, *Frankie the Walk 'N Roll Dog* was published, Frankie passed the test to become a registered therapy dog. Over the next five years we visited over 450 schools, libraries and organizations, and while most of these were in person in Wisconsin, we also used Skype to share Frankie's message to those in other states and Canada.

We also made weekly trips to one of the local facilities that served those in need—usually a nursing home, hospital or hospice. In total, there were more than two-hundred fifty visits and every time Frankie and I met with young children, the elderly, sick, or someone transitioning, it served as a reminder of what was truly important.

I also found myself in a personal space I'd never been in before, despite many years of searching. Frankie helped me peel away many layers of myself—layers that had sometimes held me back from living the life I truly wanted out of fear of what others might think. Frankie's determination to live her life to the fullest taught me to stand tall in who I am. I became more confident in myself, letting go of many fears, insecurities, and shame I had carried inside me until my early forties. And caring for her, while challenging, also gave me the sense of purpose I had been seeking for years.

In 2010 my second children's book, *Frankie the Walk 'N Roll Therapy Dog Visits Libby's House,* was published. It was inspired by our many visits to a senior assisted living facility of the same name where many residents have dementia or Alzheimer's.

In 2011, I had begun to sense that Frankie was slowing down. For a long time I pushed the painful thought to the back of my mind, but as the truth tends to do, it kept resurfacing. Eventually, I came to realize that part of the reason I was pushing it away was that there was a shift in me that was also trying to surface.

Frankie had so often been a mirror to the many internal feelings I was having, even when I had difficulty acknowledging them. When I was honest with myself I knew that, like Frankie, I also wanted to slow down and enjoy more solitude in my life. But as much as I wanted that, I was also afraid. Much of my identity came from working with Frankie…who would I be when we were no longer out there, spreading our positive message?

In this state of uncertainty, I often found myself pre-grieving Frankie's death, even though as far as I knew, she was healthy. I later learned that pre-grieving feeling is a very real, very common phenomenon. The next year, I finally decided to retire Frankie as a service animal. As I vacillated back and forth in my inner world, there were many days I truly enjoyed this new slower and quieter pace. As I sat in my writing cottage, recounting our journey and watching snow falling like little whispers outside my window, I found great joy in capturing the many joyful and beautiful moments with Frankie over the past five years.

Every now and then I'd glance down to see Frankie nestled in her pink, round bed and my heart would fill with this love that felt like no other. She had certainly earned her retirement, and to see her so contented brought me a deep sense of comfort and happiness. Little did I know as I sat lost in the thoughts that spilled onto the white pages of my computer screen, that this would be Frankie's last gift to me—the gift of being my faithful friend and companion as I worked hard to complete my memoir. The week I handed the manuscript over to my editor, Frankie was diagnosed with congestive heart failure.

Many dogs do well on medication, but while I hoped the same would be true for Frankie, she declined rapidly. Though I'd known this day would come, the realization that it had arrived was beyond heart wrenching. I didn't know how I was going to say goodbye to the ten-inch-high dog who rolled through each day with gusto and had profoundly changed my life.

In the midst of this pain I recalled a promise I had made to myself seven years earlier when my chocolate Lab, Cassie Jo, passed away. I'd spent the weekend before we said goodbye crying and wallowing in my own sadness, thus missing out on those final precious hours. I had vowed that the next time a beloved companion transitioned I would be truly present for them, and for myself. Now that Frankie was about to move on, I was determined to give her a loving and grateful farewell that honored our time together.

When Frankie passed away in June of 2012, I grieved deeply. Yet I knew without a doubt that I'd want to love and care for another dachshund afflicted with IVDD. I had no way of knowing that shortly after doing so I'd find myself going through the grieving process all over again.

CHAPTER TWO

What's in a Name?

Frankie had been gone for two months when my friend Diane came to my house for a visit. We'd met in the spring of 2005, when I engaged her as a life coach. At the time, I was struggling with not feeling fulfilled and I wanted to experience more joy in my life. Through her caring, skillful, and nurturing guidance I decided I wanted to devote my time to pursue writing, specifically about dogs and the human-animal bond.

Now, as we stood in the quaint, ten-by-twelve writing cottage my husband John had built for me three years earlier I said, "You know, Diane, I truly loved my work with Frankie. I'm grateful for the life-changing experiences that happened because of her. I wouldn't trade those years for anything. But now that she's gone, I realize that at the heart of what brought me so much joy was caring for her, and helping to ensure that she lived a quality life."

She listened without interruption, just nodded supportively.

"Even if I do nothing else in my life, caring for another dachshund with disc disease is what I want."

Looking back, I realize that even as I gave voice to my aspirations, there were still many feelings I wasn't willing to deal with. For over five years I had been a teacher of sorts, using Frankie's example to share the lessons of adversity, empathy, being positive, and how we can all make a difference. This, along with being a writer, had worked beautifully; however, in the process I had tied my identity so closely to Frankie, her story, and the mission I had become so passionate about. Without her, I wasn't sure who I was or how to move forward.

For example, while I was sure I wanted to care for another IVDD dog, I was not sure I wanted to continue the work I had done with Frankie. Yet every time someone asked me what I planned to do next, I felt pressured to tell them that, yes, I would do exactly that.

I knew well enough from my past experiences, and Diane's coaching, that much of this pressure was internal. While I had come a long way in living the life I wanted, I still had moments of worrying what others thought of my choices. I realized I was in transition, yet I wasn't ready to deal with the many unanswered questions that were playing on a loop in my mind. At the moment, I just wanted to begin my search for a new little dachshund on wheels to bring into our home. To not have another doxie in my arms soon felt too unbearable—as if a piece of me was missing.

That's when I remembered the promise I had made to John: that I wouldn't begin looking for another dachshund until we returned from our vacation to Vermont. That wasn't happening until mid-October, two months away. As the days unfolded, I grew increasingly upset with myself for making a promise that now seemed impossible for me to keep. How would I ever be able to wait so long?

My other concern was how long it would take to find another disabled dachshund—probably much longer than adopting a healthy dog. I had to remind myself that I believe that things happen when they are supposed to. While my head understood this, my heart was a whole other matter.

To add to the challenge, I had certain specifications I was looking for in my next dachshund. Every day I would silently pray for a dachshund that was female, had short red hair and was between the ages of four and six. I also prayed that she please not show up until after our trip to Vermont. I realized this was a lot to ask for, but I didn't think it hurt to put my wishes out into the universe. John, who knows me well after thirty years of marriage, added his two cents, saying that when I put my mind to something there is nothing that can stop me.

By late August, I could hardly stand the anticipation. At times I was quite anxious wondering how this would all turn out. And I worried I wouldn't find the right dog that I was wishing for. Lying in bed one night, I turned on my iPad and typed Petfinder.com into the search engine. I'm just looking, I told myself as I shielded the screen from John. I knew he would be upset because of the promise I had made.

Petfinder didn't have any dachshunds that evening that matched my specifications; which is to say I didn't find any with IVDD. But there were certainly many adorable doxies waiting for new homes. I wished I could adopt them all!

Disappointed, I was about to put the iPad away when I had the idea to do a Google search. *Just maybe something would come up this way.* But when I typed "dachshunds available for adoption + IVDD," nothing came up. My heart sinking, I thought I'd never find another special needs dachshund to love.

Still, I didn't give up hope. Every night for the next few evenings I repeated my search, first on Petfinder.com, then on Google. By the end of the week my mind was working overtime, and I'd have to remind myself to be patient and that if it was meant to be it would eventually all work out. And even though

I'd not yet found my next dachshund, I began thinking of names for her.

When I got my first dachshund from a breeder in 1999, I knew I wanted a female and I wanted to name her Frankie. I had gotten the idea after seeing the movie *Frankie and Johnny*, about an ex-con who gets a job at a diner and falls in love with a beautiful but damaged waitress. I was moved by the healing effect Johnny's love had on Frankie, and I also thought it was cool and cute for a girl to have a name usually reserved for men. Now I wanted to find another sporty name for my new dog.

Nothing came to me at first, then one night, just as I was drifting off to sleep, a name finally popped into my head. Joey! For me, it brought to mind the same kind of spunky yet feminine energy as "Frankie" had in the movie. Each time I thought of the name, I pictured it as J-o-i-e, rather than the traditional spelling. For some reason it just spoke to me.

A few days later I was on a Skype call with my friend, Mary.

"I have a name for my next dachshund!" I said excitedly.

"Really?" she asked, "What is it?"

"I'm going to name her Joie!" I spelled it out for her.

"That's perfect! Do you know that in French, Joie means joy?"

Oh my gosh, I thought, I did know that, but I'd forgotten. It was confirmation that I'd found the perfect name.

After Mary and I said goodbye, I looked up the meaning of Joie on the internet. Sure enough, I found that *joie de'vivre* means *joy of living*. My insides flooded with this instant warmth of love that traveled all the way down to my toes. Joie—whenever she arrived—would certainly bring a joy back into my life that was missing since Frankie's passing. Reading this, I was more confident than ever that I would find just the right dachshund soon.

CHAPTER THREE

Breaking a Promise

September arrived, bringing with it all the glorious shades of amber, orange and yellow. As I soaked up all the beauty of my favorite time of year, I realized that the waves of grief for Frankie were much less frequent. Time was beginning to heal the ache that had been in my heart for the past few months. While I would always miss my beloved friend and partner, I was beginning to feel more like myself again. I found myself smiling more often and looking forward to vacation, which was now only one month away.

I was even becoming re-energized around my memoir. After putting the finishing touches on the manuscript, I should have moved on to the cover design, interior layout and promotion, but without Frankie here I'd found it difficult to think about the book in print. Now I felt a new stirring of excitement inside and was looking forward to finishing it once we returned from Vermont.

Five days before we were scheduled to leave, I was sitting at my desk in my writing cottage. Part of my healing process had included a return to my blog and some journaling just for me. On this warm and quiet afternoon, however, I was just scrolling through my news feed on Facebook. Through my books, blog, and work with Frankie, I had cultivated a wonderful likeminded online community, many of whom are dedicated dachshund lovers who regularly share photos of dogs in need of new homes.

As I scrolled down the page, my eyes suddenly locked on the most adorable black and tan dachshund. My heart thumping in my chest, I took in the sweet face and shiny, jet-black eyes. *Could she be the one?*

The post was a courtesy listing by Oregon Dachshund Rescue (ODR). This meant they didn't have capacity to take in the doxie but were sharing the information in hopes of helping her find a home. As I read further I saw that that dog, whose name was Mylee, was four years old and had IVDD. The post also included the name and email address of her owner, Jackie.

I sat there for a moment, trying to contain the rush of excitement. There was my promise to John to consider; plus, I didn't want to get my hopes up. Maybe Mylee was already spoken for, or perhaps Jackie just needed some guidance on how to care for her.

Over the years, I had enjoyed sharing my knowledge with others whose pets had IVDD. It was something I wished I'd had when Frankie was first diagnosed, and I was honored to be able to give people hope that with patience and the right information their pet could live a long and happy life. Bottom line: I wouldn't know the circumstances unless I reached out to Jackie.

I sent her an email referencing the Facebook post about Mylee. I didn't ask if Mylee was still available for adoption, but suggested she reach out to Dodgerslist.com for help and expert information. I explained to her that they are a dedicated organization that educates the public about IVDD, having saved the lives of many dogs afflicted with this disease. They are a wealth of information with many helpful articles and videos.

I concluded my note by saying I'd be more than happy to talk with her about IVDD and that no matter what she should not give up hope.

When two days passed without a response, I assumed she had found a home for Mylee. So I was a bit surprised when the next day I received an email from her through the contact page of my website, Joyful Paws. "I found your website through a Google search," she wrote, "I think a wheelchair might help Mylee and I'm wondering where I could get one."

A part of me was relieved that she wanted to help Mylee by purchasing a wheelchair for her. But the other part of me was a bit heartbroken that Jackie was now considering keeping Mylee. I shrugged the thought away, reminding myself that I wanted what was best for Mylee.

Jackie had included her phone number in the email. Without thinking about it, I picked up my cell phone and punched in her number. She answered on the second ring.

"Hi Jackie, my name is Barbara Techel from Joyful Paws. You sent me an email about how to get a wheelchair for Mylee?"

"Oh yes. Thank you for calling. I'm thinking a wheelchair might help her."

As I'd done with other pet owners I had counseled, I began the conversation by asking Jackie when Mylee was first diagnosed with IVDD. While there are conflicting opinions about the right time to introduce a wheelchair into the mix, I rely on the expert advice from Dodgerslist. They suggest six to eight weeks of strict cage rest after a dog "goes down" (loses the use of the back legs). Whether or not the dog has had surgery is irrelevant; they feel this time is needed to allow the back to heal. I wanted to be sure Jackie was aware of this. She told me that Mylee had gone down several months earlier, in May.

"Did she have surgery?" I asked.

"No, because we just couldn't afford it."

"I understand," I said, and I meant it. Surgery can cost anywhere from $3,500 to $10,000, depending on what part of the country you live in.

"Did you do crate rest for her?"

"Yes."

Jackie also told me that she kept a diaper on Mylee because she had lost control of her bladder and bowels—which is common in IVDD dogs. She then shared with me that she has her own business and is raising four kids.

"My husband really wants me to find a new home for Mylee. It's just too much with everything we have going on in our lives."

"Has anyone come forward for Mylee, wanting to adopt her?"

"No, not really. Well, not anyone that I've felt comfortable with so far."

I could feel my heart start to beat faster, just like it had when I first saw Mylee's delightful face a few days before. My head, on the other hand, was spinning with thoughts of my promise to John and our upcoming vacation.

Before I knew it, the words just slipped out. "Well, I'd be interested in adopting Mylee. But there is one small glitch." I quickly explained my situation to Jackie. "Do you think you could wait until we return from vacation?"

"Yes, I can wait."

My heart beat even faster. "Okay, then I'm ninety-nine percent sure I'd like to adopt Mylee, but first I need to talk with my husband. Once I've done that I'll email you and let you know for sure."

"Thank you so much, Barbara!"

As soon as we hung up, I wanted to run outside and shout at the top of my lungs that I found a new little dog to love. Then I remembered that I still had to run this by John, and the truth was I wasn't sure what his reaction would be.

I printed off the photo of Mylee from ODR's posting; then, holding it behind my back, I held my breath and headed into the house.

CHAPTER FOUR

The Plea

I found John in the kitchen, placing his mug into the microwave to reheat his coffee.

"I have something to show you," I said, still holding the photo behind my back.

"What is it?" he said, trying to peek behind me.

Apprehensively, I placed the picture on the kitchen table.

As John glanced down at it, I quietly said, "I think I found her. Her name is Mylee."

He didn't say a word, just stared at the picture for a few moments. I tried to read his face, but I couldn't tell if he was upset or just thinking about it.

It seemed like an eternity before he finally said, "I thought you said you were going to wait until after vacation. You promised." Clearly, he wasn't happy with me.

"I know. I wasn't really even looking. But I was on Facebook a few days ago and read a post that she needed a new home. Besides, I told her owner that we are going away. She is willing to keep Mylee until we return."

He didn't say anything, but after being married to him all these years I knew not push the idea any further. John liked to process things in his own way, and I needed to give him the time to do that. Without another word, I left the room; I also left Mylee's picture on the table.

I returned to my writing cottage, but instead of sitting at the computer I plopped down in the oversized peach wicker chair and stared out the window at the garden. I knew it was more than just a timing issue with John. When Frankie became paralyzed it wasn't easy. We both had to adjust to a new way of life, and if I adopted another special needs dog we would have to do it all over again.

Of course, it hadn't come as a complete shock to John. Knowing Frankie wouldn't live forever and that I would eventually want to care for another dachshund with IVDD, I had gently brought up the subject with him on several occasions.

Most times he didn't say anything. It wasn't that he was angry; I think he was just hoping I'd change my mind. Since I knew that wasn't going to happen, I had decided to prepare him for "someday." Now that the day had arrived, I prayed with all my heart that he would be on board.

Well, just sitting there wasn't going to make the waiting easier. I needed to gather information on how I could get Mylee to Wisconsin should John agree to take her.

During my conversation with Jackie I had learned that Mylee wasn't spayed. I wasn't all that happy to hear this, as it meant an extra expense for me once she got here. But I also knew that oftentimes an animal rescue organization will cover the cost of spaying before adopting them out.

Since Oregon Dachshund Rescue had posted about Mylee, perhaps they would be willing to run her adoption too. That way I would only have to pay their adoption fee. With that thought in mind, I called ODR and left a voicemail for their president, a woman named Janelle.

An hour later, Janelle called back. She was happy to hear that I was interested in adopting Mylee, but as much as she wanted to work with me directly, she was in the middle of a family crisis. "I'm going to refer you to Linda, one of our volunteers. She will help you with all the details."

Linda turned out to be an angel in disguise. I explained my concerns about the adoption, particularly how we could transport Mylee from Washington State, where ODR was located, to me in Wisconsin. I also made it clear that I was waiting to see whether my husband would agree to the adoption. In the meantime, I told her, I wanted to get my ducks all in a row.

She said she'd be happy to handle the details, but she would need to run everything through Janelle.

"I understand," I said, "Please let her know that I'm more than willing to meet someone half way."

Just a few hours later, Linda called me back with good news. Janelle was fine with doing the adoption through ODR, and they would handle the cost to spay Mylee. Jackie just had to bring Mylee to the appointment.

Then Linda said something that struck me as rather odd. "With regards to the transportation, because Mylee has IVDD, Janelle is not comfortable with her traveling by car. She will have to travel by plane."

In my opinion, traveling by car was a better option. Flying also meant that I'd have to pay for a roundtrip ticket to Washington State. It wasn't an expense I'd planned on, but I wasn't going to let it stop me from adopting Mylee. I agreed, and Linda told me we'd work out all the details once I had definitely decided to take her. Or, more accurately, once John had decided.

Patience hasn't always been my strong suit, and by the following morning I was already starting to feel nervous. I tried to work on a project in my writing cottage, but I just couldn't concentrate. I knew I needed to brooch the subject with John again and fill him in on what I had found out from ODR. I hoped it would make a difference.

I found him in his office, hunched over his computer.

"Do you have a minute?"

"Sure," he said, turning around in his chair, "what's up?"

I hesitated for a moment. While I had nothing to lose by asking, I felt like I had everything to lose if we didn't agree on adopting Mylee. "Well, I wanted you to know I gathered more information about Mylee."

He didn't say anything, but he didn't look away either. I explained to him that Mylee needed to be spayed and this would be done while we were on vacation. I told him ODR would cover the cost of surgery.

"It's perfect timing, really. She'll need time to heal so we wouldn't be able to pick her up until after we get back."

John was quiet for a few moments, then finally said, "Okay," though I wasn't sure if he was saying okay about the information or okay to go ahead and adopt Mylee.

"Also, Janelle, the owner of Oregon Dachshund Rescue, doesn't want Mylee to travel by car. She'll need to be flown here."

"Will you fly there to get her?" he asked.

Oh wow, I'm making progress! I thought. But I didn't want to get too excited yet.

"No. Wait until you hear this! Linda, the volunteer I've been talking with from ODR, has generously offered to fly Mylee here to us."

"Wow. That is really nice of her."

"I know. Isn't it wonderful?"

I still wasn't sure, or perhaps I was just too afraid of jinxing anything, but I was pretty sure John was on board now. Still, I made my final plea in case my hunch was wrong.

"I really need you to try and understand how important

this is to me, John. It would mean so much to me to care for another special needs dog. It fulfills me on so many different levels and it makes me happy to give a dog in need a good life."

"I know," he said. "I'm just thinking about the promise you made. I really want our vacation to be just you and me this time."

I understood. I really did. While I'd loved traveling with Frankie, it always came with extra worries and concerns.

"I feel the same way," I said truthfully, "But this all seems to be working out with Mylee. We can go on our vacation, and when we return home we will have a new little dog to love."

Smiling, he wrapped an arm around my waist and pulled me toward him. "Well, since you put it that way, I'm fine with it."

When I heard the magic words, I started jumping up and down. "I have to go call Jackie and Linda right away and tell them it's a go!"

I walked back to John and squeezed him tightly. "Thank you so much for understanding my heart. I love you so much!"

"I love you, too."

John smiled as I skipped out of his office.

CHAPTER FIVE

Two Paws Up

Linda had barely uttered the word hello when I blurted out, "Hi Linda! It's Barb. It's a go! John said yes!"

"Aww, that's great!"

Linda confirmed that spaying Mylee would be done with ODR's veterinarian, and that he would also do a complete checkup to ensure that other than the IVDD she was healthy.

"Once that is all done, and everything goes smoothly, I'll book a flight to Wisconsin."

"Thank you so much, Linda, for all your help. You don't know how much it means to me."

"I'm happy to help knowing that Mylee will have a good home," she said. "I'll stay in touch. Enjoy your vacation."

"I sure will. Thank you again for everything!"

After hanging up with Linda, I called Jackie to tell her the good news.

"Oh, thank you so much," she said, "I really wish I could keep her. But I think she will have a better life with you."

My heart flooded with relief. I hadn't realized how worried I was that she might have changed her mind.

I told her that from this point on I would be in contact with Linda as Mylee went through her surgery. All she needed to do was get Mylee to ODR's vet for the procedure. She assured me that she would. I hung up the phone, bursting with happiness, yet at the same time I felt awful for Jackie. Clearly she'd had to make a very difficult decision.

Two days later, we set off for Vermont.

The birds weren't even awake when we hopped into the car at four a.m. John and I had packed the car the night before, so all I had to do was settle into the passenger seat with my pillow and blanket and a cup of orange spice tea. I was too excited to sleep, though. I was about to head to a state I had dreamed of visiting for many years, and when I returned, I would be making a trip to the airport to pick up Mylee. Life couldn't have felt any sweeter, and I planned on relishing every moment of this newfound joy.

About a half-hour later, we were coasting along on the open highway. It was still dark, and as I gazed out the window I saw only the headlights of the occasional car travelling in the other direction. Suddenly a feeling of panic came over me. Had I forgotten something? I didn't say anything to John, just wracked my brain for what I might have left behind.

It didn't take too long to realize that what I was missing was Frankie. We hadn't travelled often, but whenever we did, she was there, nestled in her car seat in the back.

Even though I knew Frankie wasn't really *here* with us, I had the urge to turn around and look into the back seat. *Oh Frankie, I miss you,* I said to myself.

It was an ache that only showed up every now and then these days. It passed quickly and I was left with a smile on my face, giving thanks for all that Frankie was, and continues to be, for me. I also couldn't help but wonder if my thinking of her in that moment was a sign from her letting me know she was okay. Just maybe, it was her way of giving me and John the "two paws up" that we were going on a much-needed vacation…and that we were adopting Mylee. My heart thumped a bit harder in my chest, another sign that Frankie was indeed assuring me that allowing myself to love again was a beautiful way in which to honor her.

It was around ten a.m. on the second day of our trip. We had stopped for gas and as I waited for John to fill the tank, my cell phone rang. My heart skipped a beat when I recognized Linda's number. She was calling to let me know that Mylee had arrived at the vet's office for the spaying and examination.

"She needs a dental, Barb, and the vet said that two teeth may need to be extracted. While ODR will cover the cost of cleaning Mylee's teeth, they don't cover the cost of extractions. The vet estimates it will cost about $175 per tooth."

"I see," I said. It was a lot of money. I wondered whether Jackie would consider paying for it, or at least splitting the cost with me.

When I asked Linda, she told me she'd first check with Janelle just to be sure ODR wouldn't cover it. She promised to call me back.

About an hour later my phone was ringing again. ODR would cover the cost should the teeth need to come out. That afternoon she called a third time to tell me the teeth didn't have to be extracted after all! The spay procedure had gone well; Mylee was resting comfortably and would be going home with Jackie later in the day.

I sighed with relief, glad the situation had been resolved before we got to Vermont and officially began our vacation. I was pretty sure my promise to John included not obsessing about Mylee while we were away.

A few hours later, I saw the "Welcome to Vermont" sign. While I had often read about—and seen photos of—the beauty of Vermont in the fall, I had no idea I was about to be transported to what would feel like another realm.

The view of the mountains as we descended into the valley took my breath away. I couldn't take in fast enough the vast stunning array of bright yellows, warm oranges and burnt reds. My heart was filled with gratitude for this beautiful land we were about to explore, and at the same time, I felt like I was coming home.

A few glorious minutes later, we pulled up to the brick red cottage with white shutters we had rented for the week. We found the key where the owners said it would be and went inside to check things out. It was immaculate, and even lovelier than I imagined, with a small screened-in porch and a darling galley kitchen flanked by a small dining area. There was even a wood-burning stove sitting in the corner.

I especially loved the cove window in the dining area. It looked out over the side yard, which was fenced in and where many leaves already carpeted the ground. There was a small drop leaf table next to the window and on the shelf of the window were some artificial flowers, knickknacks and a vintage porcelain teapot. It was the perfect spot to place my laptop. I pictured myself sitting there each evening, chronicling the day's events in a blog post.

We spent the next few hours settling in—first unpacking our things, then heading to the local market for eggs, milk, bread and other staples. After a quick bite to eat at a nearby restaurant, we decided to turn in early. We had been travelling for two days and wanted to make sure we rested up before embarking on our sightseeing plans. As I slipped into bed, I marveled how at home I felt in the cozy cottage. I was asleep before my head hit the pillow.

CHAPTER SIX

Anticipation

I was awoken the next morning by a warm sunbeam streaming through the window and onto my face. I stretched, then glanced over at the clock on the nightstand. It was only six-thirty a.m. and John was still sleeping beside me.

It was so snug under the quilt of evergreen, burgundy, and golden yellow that part of me wanted to stay in bed and read all day. But then I started thinking of all the places I wanted to see while we were here.

A sudden movement under the blankets startled me from my thoughts. It was John, pushing up the blankets and quilt from underneath. I lay still and tried not to giggle. He was mimicking how dachshunds love to push their snouts up and down, creating a hollow spot where they can burrow deep down under the blankets. He had done it before.

"Joie, is that you?" John said, "Is that a wiener dog trying to snuggle with us?"

Finally I rolled over and smiled. "So I guess I'm not the only one excited about bringing home a little dachshund, huh?"

His mouth curled up in a half grin. "Maybe."

"Well, you're not fooling me. I think perhaps you are anticipating the arrival of Joie as much as I am."

He didn't say anything, but his smile grew wider. I knew right then and there that Mylee—or Joie as I had already begun to think of her—would soon make her way right into his big, soft heart.

For the next nine days we explored the beauty of Vermont, including Robert Frost's home and the many covered bridges. My favorite, though, was the historical society in West Battleboro. The Tasha Tudor Museum, which is housed on the second floor of the building, has only two tiny rooms, but it transported me into the eccentric and delightful life of the famous children's book author and illustrator.

I had learned about Tudor while perusing a 2008 issue of Victorian Magazine just a few weeks before we left for Vermont. She had passed away that year at the age of ninety-two and there was a short write-up about her.

Perhaps it was the way she was dressed in the photo—in a frock from a long-ago era—that initially intrigued me, but it was the fact that she was a children's book writer that made me want to know more about her.

Through a search on the internet and several library books, I learned that she was a woman who truly marched to the beat of her own drum. Tudor, who claimed to be the reincarnation of nineteenth century sea captain's wife, dressed and behaved as though as she was still living during that time—she raised farm animals, made her own clothes, and even lived without electricity and running water for a time. Somehow, she also managed to raise four children and write and illustrate numerous books.

Like me, Tudor was devoted to short-legged, long-backed dogs, though in her case it was Corgis. Over the course of her lifetime she had thirteen, many of whom ended up in her children's stories, including her favorite, Corgiville Fair.

I was delighted to find that the trip to the museum included a forty-five-minute documentary in which Tudor gave a rare interview. As John and I sat in two rocking chairs and watched the DVD, I was utterly mesmerized. Tasha was one of the most authentic women I had ever seen; it radiated from every fiber of her being. Oh, how I would have loved to meet her!

When the interviewer pointed out that her lifestyle was a lot of (unnecessary) hard work, Tudor replied, "I don't feel like it's work. I feel like I've been on a vacation my whole life."

So much about Tasha deeply resonated with me. I too loved my own home and enjoyed spending a lot of time alone; I also preferred living a more simplified life, and Tasha's philosophy about not getting caught in the traps of consumerism and commercialism was very appealing.

When asked how she felt about dying, Tasha replied, "I think it will be quite exciting." She was certain she would be going back to the 1830s, where she belonged. It made the hairs on my arms stand up.

As I listened to Tasha and watched her give a tour of her secluded property, New England style home, lavish gardens, and barn with the goats, doves, and chickens, it was like I was being transported back in time. When the documentary was over, it took me a few minutes to come back to reality. I had this deeply comforted feeling, like a big warm, blanket had been wrapped around my body; I wanted it never to end.

Unfortunately, the visit to the museum, and to Vermont, flew by all too quickly. The feeling as our vacation came to a close was bittersweet—I didn't want to leave, yet I was anxious to return home knowing I would soon be holding Joie in my arms.

We didn't have anything planned for our last day, so we decided to take a leisurely drive in the country. The winding, picturesque roads dotted with farms took my breath away. But it was the mountains serving as the backdrop of vast open fields that touched a place deep in my heart. In a way, the mountains had become like dear old friends, and I didn't want to leave them.

The next day, I quickly dressed and went for a walk around the neighborhood. I had done this most mornings and had begun to feel really connected. On my last stroll along the charming streets I tried to absorb the scenery deep into my memory cells so I could recall it anytime I wanted.

When I got back, John had most of the car packed; it was time to head out. As we drove down the short gravel driveway, the sun streaming in the car windows, I turned and gave the quaint red house a little wave. "Goodbye," I whispered sadly.

My melancholy only increased as the glorious mountains began to fade from view. For years I'd felt drawn to Vermont, and this trip had only confirmed that connection. But as hard as it was to leave, I made the conscious choice to be grateful for the experience and look forward to Joie's arrival. A new chapter was about to begin.

Two days later, when we finally arrived in our small town, I was both surprised and thrilled to see the brilliant orange, red and gold leaves on the trees. We had left Vermont in peak season and had come home to the same; it almost felt like an extension to our vacation.

As soon as we opened the front door we were greeted by Kylie, our seven-year old yellow English Labrador.

Patting the top of her head, I said, "Hey girl! I missed you. I'll bet Grandpa P spoiled you while we were gone, huh?"

Kylie, such a gentle soul, has always gone with the flow, even when things were toughest with Frankie. She is my rock, able to ground me with her presence alone. I've often thought about how she was forced to play second-fiddle to Frankie, but she never seemed to be bothered by it. Kylie's sweet, carefree way made me love her all the more; it also made me feel much more comfortable about bringing a new special needs doxie into our home.

The following day I jumped enthusiastically back into my work. I wrote a post for my blog, then made a list of tasks I needed to accomplish in order to complete my memoir, such as finalizing the book cover design and hiring someone to put together the interior layout. Thinking about my to-do list made me even more excited about everything that was unfolding.

Before I got too involved with all that needed to be done, I took a moment to email Linda from Oregon Dachshund Rescue and let her know we had returned home. Mostly, though, I wanted to hear about her flight details.

Linda responded almost immediately. On Friday, about a half-hour before she boarded the plane, Jackie would deliver Mylee/Joie to her at Sea TAC airport. She would arrive in Wisconsin at five p.m.

Now all I had to do was keep calm and prepare for the new little love of my life to arrive. Easier said than done!

CHAPTER SEVEN

Home Sweet Home

That Friday afternoon, John and I set off on another adventure—we were going to Milwaukee Mitchell airport to meet Linda and Joie's flight. As he eased the car onto the highway, I found myself grinning like a fool. I could hardly believe that in a few hours I would be holding a little dachshund in my arms again.

A few moments into the drive I received a text from Linda. It was a photo of Joie snuggled in her bright yellow carrier. Her tiny head was sticking out the top and she had a stuffed blue and pink bone in her mouth. My heart melted at the sight of her, and I couldn't help but feel terrible for Jackie at having to part with this pretty, precious pup.

We arrived at the airport at about three, two hours before Linda and Joie were scheduled to land. We found a restaurant and enjoyed some beverages and appetizers to pass the time, then walked through the terminal until we found a spot to wait for the flight.

As we sat there, a couple walked by with a big, lanky, yellow Labrador. He had the droopiest face with the prettiest brown eyes. He was wearing a service dog vest, and as much as I wanted to pet him, I respected the fact that he was working.

The couple and the beautiful dog sat down a few feet from us. A few moments later, two young girls walked by. When they saw the dog they stopped and asked if they could pet him.

The man told them they could, then I heard him say that the dog wasn't on duty; in fact, the person the dog had been in service to had passed away after just nine months. The dog was being transported back home to the woman who had originally trained him.

My heart went out to the dog for having just lost his friend. At the same time, I was in complete admiration for how he had made the person's life easier, even if for only a short time. The girls patted the dog on the head one last time, thanked the couple, and continued on their way.

After they left, I couldn't help but walk over to the couple.

"I just love dogs," I said, "May I pet him?"

The man smiled and said, "Of course."

"What's his name?"

"Buster."

"Oh, that's a perfect name. It fits him well."

I've always been amazed by the way dogs open our world and give us the confidence to meet people we may not have otherwise. Thanks to my work with Frankie, I'd met some wonderful people along the way that are now treasured friends.

As I stroked Buster's soft head, I told the couple I was there to pick up my own dog—a female dachshund with special needs who was flying in with a volunteer from Washington State. A woman two seats down from us overheard me and said, "I love dachshunds. I miss mine and can't wait to get home to him."

"I understand," I said. "It's hard to be away from them, isn't it? I'm excited to get my new little one soon!"

"I can't wait to see her. When is she arriving?"

"Just a few more moments," I said.

Here we all were, just a small group of strangers who in a matter of minutes had bonded over our love of dogs. Just then I heard over the PA system that flight #512 had landed.

This also meant it was time for Buster to catch his flight. Just as he and his temporary guardians went to get in line, I heard my phone ding. Linda was texting to tell me she was making her way off the airplane!

As John and I walked to the end of the terminal, I fought the urge to cross the line and run to meet her. John stood a few feet behind me with camera in hand, ready to capture the special moment as I met Joie for the first time.

My eyes scanned the crowd of deplaning passengers, looking for someone who resembled the photo Linda had sent of herself a few days earlier. Face after face passed by me, until finally I saw in the distance a woman who I thought might be her. When my line of vision was clear, I looked to see what she was carrying and sure enough, she had the regulation bright yellow carrier in her left hand. It was Joie, my precious cargo!

My eyes instantly filled with tears as a wave of bitter-sweet emotions washed over me. Even as I waited to meet Joie, Frankie's image flashed across my mind. I would always love and miss her, but it was now time for me to experience a new love.

Suddenly, Linda was standing in front of me. I reached out and hugged her, careful not to jolt the carrier in her hand. Smiling, she set it down, and I immediately dropped to my knees right next to it. I thought my heart would burst as she slowly unzipped the carrier; then, just when I couldn't stand the wait any longer, Joie's head popped out the top of the soft-sided kennel. All the tears I had been trying to hold in came flooding out.

As I gently cupped my hands around her sweet face, I realized she was tinier than she had appeared in the photos Jackie sent me.

"Oh Joie, I love you," I said, then, placing my hands around the middle of her body, I scooped her into my arms and held her close against my chest. My heart was home again.

As Joie and I got acquainted, Linda started to pull out the adoption paperwork and her medical records. We had some business to take care of and, since her return flight was leaving in thirty minutes, not much time to do it.

After I'd signed the paperwork to make it all official, I reached into my bag and pulled out an envelope and handed it to Linda. Inside was a card and some money to show my appreciation that she'd given up her Saturday to fly Joie to me.

Taking the envelope, she smiled. "You're welcome. I was happy to do it."

We hugged once more, then it was time for Linda to get back in line, the now empty carrier in her hand. She turned one last time and waved goodbye, then headed for the security line.

As John and I headed back through the terminal, I remembered the woman I had spoken to earlier, the one with her own dachshund. When I looked over to the waiting area, I spotted her right away and walked toward her.

Tears sprung to her eyes as I knelt down in front of her with Joie in my arms.

"Meet my new little friend, Joie."

Reaching her hand out to pat the side of Joie's body, she said, "It was so sweet to witness you meeting her for the first time. She is really darling."

"She is, isn't she?" I said, proudly. I felt so incredibly lucky to know that she was now mine.

After introducing her to Joie, John handed me our own soft-sided black dog carrier. I would have loved to keep her in my arms, but it was against airport regulations. I knelt on the floor and gently placed my sweet girl inside.

As we began walking through the airport, Joie was a little fidgety; luckily it was only a short distance to the parking lot. Still, I held her as close to my chest and talked to her. "We will be in the car soon, sweetie. Then I will hold you again."

A few minutes later we reached our car, and true to my word, I set the carrier down next to the passenger side, unzipped it, and scooped Joie out. John opened the car door for me as I carefully climbed into the passenger seat.

When we were settled in I reached into my bag and pulled out the harness Frankie always used to wear. It had a convenient loop on the back, and after putting it on Joie, I slid my seatbelt through the loop and then around me. We were both safely buckled in.

As John eased the car into highway traffic, I saw Joie's eyes slowly close, only to flicker open again. She had had a long day and now she was fighting hard to stay awake. Within minutes, though, I felt her body relax even more into my arms, and when I looked at her sweet face again I saw she was fast asleep. She already felt safe and contented with me!

I knew the feeling. I had known Joie less than an hour and already my heart was exploding with love for her. It was a raw, rainy October day, but with all the warmth radiating from my heart I barely noticed.

A little over an hour later, we were walking through the kitchen door off the garage. As always, Kylie was right there to greet us, her tail wagging a hundred miles a minute, her snout turned up toward the bundle in my arms.

I immediately knelt down in front of her so she could

investigate this new addition to the household. Kylie pressed her snout to Joie's body and sniffed.

"This is your new little sister, Joie. You must be gentle with her, okay?" Kylie's tail kept wagging as if in agreement.

I set Joie down on the large, pink, soft dog pillow across from Kylie's kennel—a place that Kylie and Frankie had often snuggled together—then I sat down, placing my body between Joie and Kylie.

"It's okay, Kylie. You can come over and say hi to Joie."

She approached slowly and then began sniffing Joie from the top of her head all the way down to the end of her tail. Joie patiently endured the investigation, which lasted all of a minute. Apparently, Kylie had decided she was okay with everything because she walked to her kennel, went inside and lay down. I took it as a good sign.

As the excitement of the day wound down, I suddenly realized how exhausted I was. One look at John told me he felt the same, so I decided to keep dinner simple. I popped a pizza in the oven and as it baked I got Joie's bed ready for the night. John had placed one condition on our getting a new dog: she couldn't sleep with us. Frankie had always slept in our bed, and as much as we loved it, we had both realized over the past few months how much better we were sleeping without her. I didn't know where Joie had slept at Jackie's, but I put her kennel right next to my side of the bed, hoping it would comfort her to know I was nearby.

After we finished dinner, I sat on the sofa in the living room with Joie in my lap. I told her how happy I was to have her in my life. "I love you so much, Joie. I promise I'll do my best to give you a good life."

By this time Joie's eyes were half-mast and mine were drooping as well, so I walked into our bedroom and gently placed her in the kennel. She looked up at me questioningly with her soft, jet-black eyes.

"It's okay, Joie," I murmured as I climbed into bed. It felt like a warm hug. "This is your new home. Sleep tight."

Within minutes, we were all fast asleep.

CHAPTER EIGHT

Startling Discovery

The next morning I was awoken by the sounds of birds chirping. I sat up in bed, smiling when I saw that the sun was shining brightly—a drastic change from the cold, damp weather the day before.

Joie must have heard me stir, because when I peeked into her kennel I was greeted by her sweet face looking up adoringly at me. I knew the feeling.

"I didn't hear a peep out of you all night. Does this mean you are happy to be here in your new home?"

Next to me, John stretched and sat up. As he headed to the kitchen to make coffee, I lifted Joie out of her kennel and off to the bathroom so I could express her bladder. Having experienced this with Frankie for six years, it had become like second nature to me. And just like I had trained Frankie to balance her front paws on the rim of the toilet seat, I could tell Joie would take to it as well. I gently squeezed her bladder over the bowl and flushed.

A few minutes later I was sitting across from John at the kitchen table, with Joie nestled on my lap. Kylie sat contently on the olive green rug by the front door, gazing out into the yard.

"We need to build a fire," I said. "We probably won't be able to enjoy too many more before it gets cold."

John and I loved our deck and, weather permitting, spent as much time out there as possible. Our favorite thing to do was sit and be with the dogs around the small, red clay chiminea, or freestanding fireplace.

John leaned over and peered at my lap. "Would you like that, Joie? I bet you don't even know what a chiminea is, but I think you'll like it."

I thought so too, and as much as I looked forward to having Joie join us in this ritual, I was still a little nervous about how she would adjust to our home. I also knew I wouldn't find out by keeping her on my lap all day. After a few moments, I cautiously sat her down on the hardwood floor so she could check out her new surroundings.

I'd known ever since seeing the Facebook post that Joie had IVDD and the paralysis in the hind legs commonly caused by it. However, I was surprised to see that she also seemed to be having trouble holding her *front* limbs in place. Within seconds of my putting her down, they slid out to either side of her body, like Bambi on ice.

Trying not to be alarmed, I picked her up and placed her on the rug near Kylie to see if it made any difference. While it did seem to help somewhat, her front limbs were still splayed out to the sides, making her sit in a wide stance.

I turned to John, who also watching. "That's not normal."

"Yes, that looks odd."

"I'll call Dr. M on Monday and see how fast I can get Joie in there."

"That's a good idea."

Dr. M, a vet I found when Frankie went down years before, specializes in helping IVDD dogs. At a time when I was overwhelmed and wondering how I could help Frankie, she had been a great blessing. She provided information on caring for, and living with, a dog with disc disease, and taught me different exercises I could do for Frankie to keep muscle atrophy to a minimum. I had no doubt that she would be able to guide me with Joie as well.

That evening, John and I sat in our periwinkle Adirondack chairs, enjoying the crackling fire in the chiminea. The season had definitely taken a turn. The air had a crisp feel to it, the light was fading earlier each evening, and many leaves from our locust tree had already fallen onto our deck too. Tonight was noticeably cooler as well, but that may have had more to do with Lake Michigan than any seasonal change. Although we live about twenty-five miles west of the lake, any wind coming off it put an extra chill in the air. This was the case tonight, and while Kylie welcomed the cooler weather, the rest of us had to bundle up—John and I in heavy sweatshirts, and Joie in a purple fleece coat that had belonged to Frankie. To make sure she was extra snug, I also wrapped a big, thick blanket around her.

With Joie on my lap and John and Kylie beside me, I felt a warm sense of peace wash over me. It was a feeling of contentment I hadn't experienced since Frankie died.

Next to me, John also seemed at peace as he gazed into the burning embers. I smiled to myself, remembering the fuss he'd made when I first brought the chiminea—a hand-me-down from my mom—to our home. John took one look at it, grumbled something about it being too heavy to carry to the back of the house, and left it in the garage, where it sat for the next two years. I recalled how disappointed I was that he didn't see the benefit of it, and how pleased I was when one day he suddenly had this "epiphany" that it would be a good thing for us to have on our deck. Since then we had been getting great enjoyment from it—perhaps John even more so than me.

It wasn't always easy for John to relax. Running his own construction business with a crew of three guys and the amount of hard work it took to land jobs was often stressful. The chiminea had become a meditation of sorts for him—it helped him to let go of concerns for a while and just be. For me, this was more important than my enjoyment of the chiminea itself.

As I thought more about our life, a warm, tingling feeling of gratitude came over me. I had John and my work, Kylie and our lovely home, and now there was Joie—my *joie de vivre*—to love as well. Even though I was concerned about her front legs, I tried to not worry too much. No doubt Dr. M would soon answer many questions, and Joie would get the help she needed.

I called right after breakfast the next morning and was relieved when the receptionist told me Dr. M had an opening that week.

That Thursday I made the two-hour drive to the office and was greeted by a vet tech I had never met before. Her name was Sarah, and her kind, friendly nature immediately put me at ease. I followed her to an exam room, then sat down on the bench against the wall and settled Joie on my lap while Sarah sat down at a computer to start her patient file.

While I told her what I knew about Joie's health history, it came up that she wasn't my first dog with IVDD. When I told her about Frankie, Sarah's smile grew broader.

"I have a dog in a wheelchair too," she said, "His name is Wicket, and he's famous too, just like your Frankie was."

"Really?" I said, leaning forward in my seat. For although I regularly saw other dogs in wheelchairs on Facebook and in different articles, I'd never personally met someone who had a dog in a wheelchair.

"Yes, he's in my dad's T.V. commercial," she said.

I knew right away what commercial she was talking about!

It was for, of all things, a law office, and I had often wondered whether the dog really needed the wheelchair or was just "acting" for the commercial.

"That's *your* dog?" I asked in amazement, "And is your dad the lawyer?"

"Yup! It's Wicket and my dad, alright."

"Wow, that's so cool. Does Wicket have disc disease?"

"No. I was in a car accident and Wicket was with me. We were both badly hurt, and he became paralyzed as a result."

"I'm so sorry to hear that, but it's beautiful that you've given him another chance at life."

She nodded. "I'm really grateful that wheelchairs for pets are an option!"

As we bonded over our love for wheelie dogs, I told her about National Walk 'N Roll Dog Day, the special day I'd founded in memory of Frankie and to honor all dogs in wheelchairs. It was the best way for me to continue the work I'd done with Frankie. It was also the best way to spread the word that dogs in wheelchairs could live quality lives.

"You should check out the Facebook page," I told her, "And please share a picture of Wicket on my timeline so others can see him too."

"I sure will," she said, "Oh, I can't wait to go on Facebook when I get home tonight."

Beaming from ear to ear, I mentioned that since Frankie's passing I had also started The Frankie Wheelchair Fund. Many of her fans had sent money in her honor, which I used to help six small dogs get wheelchairs. They were dogs who might otherwise not have been able to have one, either because they were in rescue awaiting new homes or their families couldn't afford them. Knowing I had made in a difference in their lives was an incredible feeling.

"Wow," Sarah said, clearly moved. "That really is special."

After asking a few more questions about Joie, she told me to make myself comfortable and that the doctor would be in shortly.

True to her word, Sarah returned with Dr. M a few minutes later. The vet was just as I remembered her, with short, dishwater blond hair and a petite frame. She also had the same gentle spirit that had calmed me the first time I brought Frankie in.

"It's nice to see you again," she said as we shook hands, "I was so sorry to hear about Frankie."

"Thank you. It was difficult, but I'll always feel very blessed to have had her in my life. She taught me so much."

Dr. M nodded understandingly, then glanced at Joie. "So, this is the new pup you adopted?"

"Yes, this is Joie. I adopted her from a rescue organization out of Oregon."

"It's wonderful that you decided to adopt another dog with IVDD," she said. "Well, let's have a look at Joie. Why don't you set her on the floor so I can see how she gets around."

I noted the cement floor and hesitated. "Joie will likely have a hard time holding herself up on the slippery surface. It's part of the reason I'm here today. I'm concerned about her front legs."

Dr. M turned to Sarah. "Will you get that carpet sample we have in the back?"

Sarah hurried from the room, returning a moment later with a roll of carpet the size of a runner. Dr. M and I moved to the side of the room as Sarah rolled it out, then I stepped forward and carefully set Joie down in the middle.

As Joie began to sniff and explore, I explained to Dr. M how her front legs tend to splay out when was on a smooth surface like tile or hardwood flooring.

Dr. M nodded thoughtfully. "Yes, I can see that something isn't quite right just by observing her on the carpeting. That's so peculiar."

She then gently picked Joie up and placed her back down in a different position. She did this several times. Then she moved her hands up and down Joie's back, slowly feeling each part of her spine.

I said, "I don't know much about her history. I'm not sure how and why she was diagnosed with IVDD. I'm also not sure where her rupture occurred because I didn't want to press Jackie for the information. What I do know is that Joie went down last May and did not have surgery because the family couldn't afford it. I also don't know how long she was crate-rested."

Dr. M continued to examine Joie's spine.

"She can't control her bladder," I continued, hoping to provide any information that might shed light on what was going on, "and she wore a diaper when she lived with her other family. I've been expressing her bladder several times a day so she no longer needs it."

When Dr. M still didn't say anything, I asked, "Just from examining Joie, can you tell where her rupture may have occurred?"

"Yes. It seems to have happened between T-12 and T-13."

"Hmmm. That's where Frankie's rupture was too."

"It's a common spot," she replied.

I had enough experience with the disease to know that sometimes a disc could just rupture without any trauma or known cause. Still, I was curious what had happened to Joie.

"I'm not sure if she fell or if the rupture just happened…" I trailed off, hoping she would fill in the blank.

Finally, Dr. M gently picked Joie up off the floor. "Well, I must admit I've never seen anything like what's going on with her front legs. As far as the rupture, though, I do believe it may have been caused by trauma."

"What do you mean?" I asked, suddenly concerned that she might have been abused.

"Well, she could have fallen or possibly been dropped by accident."

"I see." While I was glad the doctor didn't feel that someone had intentionally hurt Joie, the truth was no matter what had happened we now needed to move forward. "What can I do to help her?"

"You will need to do some physical therapy with her, every day. I had thought perhaps swimming therapy, but after examining her, I think we should start with some gentle range of motion and passive exercises."

"Okay." I smiled. "Well, I've certainly done that before."

"Great. Let's begin by placing her front legs in the correct position while at the same time holding her back end in place."

As Dr. M demonstrated, Joie's front limbs began to slide out to the sides again.

"I think I may have something to help with that," she said, turning to a cabinet behind her. I saw her pull something out and when she turned back to me she was holding two small orange booties. "These are Pawz Dog Boots," she said, handing me one, "They're made of breathable rubber and are waterproof."

I looked down at the tiny boot in my hand. "It almost looks like a balloon."

"Exactly," Dr. M replied, then sure enough, she stretched one end of the boot she was holding, similar to the way one would stretch the opening of a balloon before blowing air into it. She slipped the boot over Joie's right front paw, then took the other one back from me and did the same on the left paw.

This time, when she set Joie back down on the carpet and positioned her as she had before, there was a noticeable difference. Joie now had better traction. Her front legs were staying in place!

"Wow! Those work really nice," I said.

Smiling, Dr. M said, "I have recommended them to many of my patients. They were originally designed to use when walking dogs outside to protect their paws in inclement weather, but I've found they help in other ways, too."

Dr. M continued to move Joie through different positions, with me copying each move to make sure I was doing it right. It felt good to be taking positive action that would hopefully help Joie.

"What about a wheelchair?" I asked, "I still have Frankie's, and I'm sure with a little help from Eddie's Wheels my husband John could adjust it to fit Joie."

"Let's wait on the wheelchair for now. We really need to work on building up Joie's upper body strength first."

"Of course, that makes sense," I agreed.

Most of the exercises were easy enough to do, and just like with Frankie, I found it a joy to do them with Joie now. There was one particular exercise though that was a bit more challenging than the others, mostly because Joie couldn't seem to sit still. I had actually noticed this the first few days I had her. It was as if she couldn't balance, and her spine was always in motion, trying to adjust. She oftentimes shifted back and forth in small, but noticeable sways from side to side. I asked Dr. M why this might be.

"It appears that one side of her body is more compromised than the other. She is weaker on the left side, and this makes it very difficult for her to sit still."

When I heard this, my heart went out to Joie. How uncomfortable it must be to not be able to settle down. However, I had also noticed that when Joie was lying down the constant back and forth motion of her spine stopped.

"I think for now it's best to work on the exercises," Dr. M advised. Once she is stronger, you can introduce the wheelchair. See how that goes and if you need to come back again, I'd be happy to see her."

"Sounds like a plan," I said as I stood to leave.

"By the way, Sarah told me about the special day you started, and the fund to help other paralyzed dogs get wheelchairs."

"Yes. I wanted to carry on the work I began with Frankie and thought that was a good way to do it."

"Well, we hold a few events each year to raise money for animal causes. Maybe we can work together in the future to help dogs in need of wheelchairs."

"Really? That would be wonderful. Thank you so much!"

"Of course. Well, it was great meeting Joie and seeing you again. Keep me posted and don't hesitate to call with any questions or concerns."

"You bet. Thank you for all your help today."

As I drove home, I thought back to everything Dr. M and I had discussed, from the possible causes of Joie's paralysis to the little orange booties and exercises, and finally to Dr. M's suggestion that we might work together in the future to help dogs in need of wheelchairs. Next to me, Joie drifted off to sleep in her car seat. As I reached over to pat her head, I silently thanked Spirit for continuing to guide me on the next phase of my mission, even if I didn't always know what that next phase would look like.

CHAPTER NINE

The Gift of Mobility

The next day I began physical therapy with Joie, and as I would soon find out, it was more challenging than it had been with Frankie.

Joie was younger than Frankie had been when she became paralyzed, and a bit more rambunctious. While Frankie would lie still as I manipulated her hind legs, Joie had a harder time sitting still. This made moving through the exercises a bit more difficult. The fact that her spine was in constant motion also made it challenging, and I soon found myself getting frustrated. But no matter how bad it got, I knew I would never give up on her. I kept working with her each day, even though it seemed like it was taking longer than I thought it should to see results.

In January, a few months after we saw Dr. M, I received a phone call from Sarah.

"Sarah! How are you? And how is Wicket doing? It's so fun to see him in the commercial now that I know who he is."

"I'm doing great and so is Wicket. The reason I'm calling is Dr. M is going to be teaching a series of pet massage classes. She will be offering a class in February, March and April."

"That's wonderful! I'd certainly like to learn. I may have to sign up for one of the classes."

"Well, the reason for my call is that in lieu of a fee Dr. M is going to ask people to donate to The Frankie Wheelchair Fund."

When I heard the news, I was speechless. When Dr. M had suggested working together in the future, I'd never anticipated something like this.

"Really?" I said after a moment, "That is so kind."

"Yes, we are really excited about the classes and we think we will have a good turnout."

"I really appreciate this, Sarah. Please thank Dr. M and let her know I'll be happy to promote the classes."

She said she would convey the message and promised to be in touch soon with the details.

After we said our goodbyes I sat at the kitchen table, my heart flooded with many different emotions. Since Frankie's passing I had missed our volunteer work, and it felt good to be making a difference in another way. Smiling, I scooped up Joie, who was sitting at my feet, and looked into her eyes.

"How would you like it if I learned to give you a massage? I bet that would feel good."

She returned my stare for a moment, then laid her head on my arm as if agreeing to what I had said. My heart melted, while my mind was already thinking about the possibilities. I had begun to see slight improvement—times when Joie seemed to hold herself up for a few seconds longer than before—and thought perhaps incorporating massage with her daily therapy might facilitate that.

A month later, Joie had definitely grown stronger. Thinking it might be time to test out Frankie's wheelchair, I retrieved it from the basement. I placed Joie's back legs through the openings of the black rubber saddle, then moved the aluminum bar from the left side of her body, over the top of her back and secured it in place with the metal pins. This would keep her body and back aligned within the wheelchair. Lastly, I put the canvas strap around the front of her chest and snapped it in place.

It was a little big on her because she was approximately four pounds lighter than Frankie, but I wanted to see if she felt comfortable in it. At first she just stood in the wheelchair, not sure of what she should do, then her front legs began to splay out to either side. It was too soon, I realized; we needed to continue to build up her muscles.

In the meantime, I emailed Eddie's Wheels and asked for suggestions on how to best adjust the wheelchair to fit Joie. Between their guidance and John's background as a machinist, he was able to make the proper adjustments.

Another two weeks went by before I tried the wheelchair again. In that time we had made significant progress. I believed her front legs were much stronger now. But just like the first time, she didn't move, just looked at me as if to say, "How do I use this thing?"

A few feet away was the basket where I kept her and Kylie's toys. I walked over and plucked out Joie's favorite— which had come with her from her previous home—and started squeaking it. She tried to move forward, but the hardwood floor was too slippery for her to gain traction. Time for Plan B.

I took Joie outside and set her down on the driveway, and again she stood there, still as a statue.

"Come on, Joie," I said as I squeaked the toy, "I know you can do it."

It only took a few more squeaks before she started to inch her way toward me. "Good job, Joie! Look at you walk!"

I had also stuffed my pocket with a few treats before we had headed outside. Once I had her walking, I stayed a few inches in front of her, placing a treat on the ground to keep her coming toward me. It worked! Before long she had walked all the way to the end of the driveway.

Seeing Joie regain her mobility brought back the same rush of joy I'd felt the first time Frankie walked after being paralyzed. After months of work, it seemed that Joie and I had truly turned a corner.

Much as I would have liked to take her outside every day, the Wisconsin winter had other ideas. Whenever possible we would go out for ten to fifteen-minute "sessions" designed to get her used to walking in her wheels. She loved exploring and eventually moved off the driveway and into the yard. The grass was a bit harder for her to maneuver around in, but it was also a great way to strengthen the muscles in her front legs.

A few weeks later I finally felt like she was strong enough to go for a longer walk. Once Joie was in her wheelchair and her leash hooked to the D-ring on the back of her harness, I turned to Kylie.

"Come on, Kylie, let's take Joie for a walk!"

I didn't have to ask twice. Kylie ran toward me, her tail wagging enthusiastically, and the three of us set off down the street.

We had only gone about two blocks when I noticed that Joie was beginning to slow down. This worried me a little, as she had taken off at high speed when we got down the driveway. Then I realized it had been eight months since she walked on her own. It was going to take a while to build her stamina back up again.

I picked her up, wheels and all, and carried her home with Kylie walking calmly beside me. We would try again tomorrow.

Before I knew it, the day of Dr. M's pet massage class had arrived.

I found myself looking forward to it even more than I thought I would. Although I loved Joie very much, we seemed to be having a hard time bonding. This odd feeling of disconnect made me sad, especially since I'd never experienced this with any of my other dogs. I hoped that if I learned to massage Joie, it would help us grow closer.

As I pulled into the parking lot of the vet clinic where the massage class was being held, I didn't give much thought to how many other dogs would be there. Jackie had told me that Joie was good around other dogs, and that had certainly been the case with Kylie.

I had no sooner taken the key out of the ignition when a woman got out of an SUV parked nearby. She opened the back and out jumped a big, beautiful German shepherd. I smiled as I thought about all the magnificent dogs I would see this morning.

Joie, who was still buckled in her car seat, apparently felt differently, because the minute she saw the dog she began barking frantically. It wasn't a bark I had heard from her before; in fact, it sounded to me like one of fear. I waited until the woman and her dog had entered the vet clinic. Sure enough, Joie stopped barking as soon as they were out of sight. I gently unhooked her from her car seat and got out of the car.

A few minutes later, I walked through the front door, with Joie gliding beside me in her wheelchair. We were met by a member of the staff who directed us to a nearby elevator. It would take us down to the lower level where the class was being held.

Joie rolled right into the elevator without hesitation; however, rolling out when we got down to the basement was another story. She wouldn't budge. I picked her up in my arms and carried her off the elevator and down the hallway.

As I walked through the door of the classroom, I saw dogs everywhere. Some big, some small, some were lying on blankets, and some sitting on tables with their owners behind them. Under most circumstances I would have been thrilled, but as soon as Joie saw the dogs she began to bark frantically again. I broke out in a nervous sweat. How in the world was this going to work out?

Just then, Sarah approached us. "Hi, Barb," she said over Joie's high-pitched barking, "We have a table near the front of the room for you and Joie. Is that okay?"

I peered over her right shoulder. "Yes, actually that looks perfect. It may help Joie to be a little further away from the other dogs. Thank you."

Indeed, she did calm down a bit as I made my way toward the table; she wasn't wiggling as much and had even stopped barking. She seemed to do better as long as she didn't see the other dogs.

When I reached our spot, I took out a blanket from my bag and laid it across the table. Then I took Joie out of her wheelchair and set her on the table, facing me.

I thought this would do the trick, but Joie wanted nothing to do with it. She tried with all her might to turn around and look behind her, then as soon as she got a glimpse of a tail or pointy ears, she busted out in a full barking episode.

My heart beat faster and I started to sweat again. I didn't know how we were going to make it through a whole ninety-minute class. We hadn't even begun and my nerves were already frazzled.

I was still trying to calm Joie down when Dr. M walked to the front of the room and asked me to tell the class about the Frankie Wheelchair Fund. While I was happy and honored to do so, I was anxious about what Joie would do.

Luckily, she stopped barking as I spoke; it was almost as if she knew it would have been inappropriate to make a scene. After I was done, Dr. M spoke for a few minutes about the benefits of massage, then demonstrated the first technique. I tried to follow along, but it was difficult, what with Joie fidgeting the whole time. I was trying to massage her and she was doing everything she could to turn around and see the other dogs. It felt like we were working against each other.

It was about a half hour into the class when Sarah, who had been walking around the room checking each person and dog, made her way over to me and Joie.

"Joie is so uncomfortable," I said. "I just don't know what to do."

"Maybe you should take her outside for a few moments. That might help."

"That's a good idea. I'll be back," I said, only too happy to take a break.

Once we were outside, I put Joie in her wheelchair and let her snorkel around in the grass while I enjoyed the feel of the sun on my face. Joie seemed to be happy and content as she explored her surroundings, and I wondered whether learning the massage techniques was the best way to meet her needs.

"You know, Joie," I said to her, "I brought you to this pet massage class because I want to do all that I can to help you feel better. I hope you can understand this. I really do love you."

I stared down at her, half-expecting a reaction, but she was too busy sniffing every blade of grass to even glance my way. After about ten minutes I decided it was time to head back inside and try again.

When I walked back into the classroom with Joie in my arms, I didn't know what to expect. Fortunately, it seemed that Joie had heard me outside, because she stayed quiet. For the duration of the class, she was much more relaxed; she even let me practice the different massage strokes on her. Seeing this made me relax as well, and I soon found that I was really enjoying this special one-on-one time with her.

When the class ended and the room began to clear, Sarah walked over to me again. "I want to send the donations home with you today, if you have a few moments to wait."

"Of course. Thank you."

While Sarah sat at a nearby desk, tallying the donations, I put Joie back in her wheelchair and allowed her to explore the now-empty room.

A few moments later Sarah let out a loud squeal. "There is over $300 here!"

"Oh wow, seriously? That is wonderful!"

She walked over and handed me a thick white envelope. "Thank you so much," I said as I pulled her into a hug, "I truly appreciate this."

"You are very welcome," she said with a smile in her voice. I knew how excited she was to help dogs who need wheelchairs.

Two more massage classes were held after that—one in March and April—and a total of $900 collected. This meant I could help give two or three more paralyzed dogs the gift of mobility with a donated wheelchair. It brought me great comfort to know that while I didn't know what was next for me and Joie, I at least knew that Frankie's legacy would continue.

CHAPTER TEN

Launch of Memories

About a month before I adopted Joie, I signed up for *The Artist's Way*, a twelve-week workshop being held at Plymouth Art Center. Based on Julia Cameron's book of the same name, the workshop claimed you can "recover your creativity from a variety of blocks, including limiting beliefs, fear, self-sabotage, jealousy, guilt, addictions, and other inhibiting forces, replacing them with artistic confidence and productivity." I was hoping it could help guide me in my search for a new direction.

When the first session began in mid-September, I immediately knew I was right where I was meant to be. I felt at home surrounded by other writers and artists. After hearing them talk about their own struggles, some of the self-doubt and worry that had been plaguing me since Frankie died began to lift.

In the coming months, the workshop and its participants would remind me that life would unfold as it was meant to and guide me through the times of uncertainty that snuck up on me quite often.

It was at times difficult to share my own story, particularly the hardship John and I endured during the financial meltdown in 2008. However, I found that in saying these things out loud and allowing myself to be vulnerable, I was able to let go of some the baggage I had been carrying around for the past few years.

Our last session came way too quickly. It was early December and just four weeks from the release of my memoir. I was excited and nervous all at the same time, which I took as a good sign. I had even found the venue for my launch. The workshop had been so enriching that I decided that Plymouth Art Center was the perfect place. Indeed, it seemed that from the moment I booked the large room for an evening at the end of February, friends and family began offering to help me in any way they could. It felt incredibly good to be in the groove of what mattered to me.

It was a bittersweet experience, though, knowing Frankie wouldn't be at my side. I was delighted that Joie would be there to share the moment, although I wasn't quite sure how she would handle a room full of people. John eased my worry somewhat by offering to take care of her for me.

A few weeks before the launch, I sat down to work on the short speech I would make that evening. I knew what I wanted to say but for some reason each time I went to type I felt like hundreds of butterflies were fluttering around in my stomach. I kept reminding myself that I'd done many presentations over the years, and that once I got talking, those butterflies would likely find a soft place to land. They always did.

I also realized that I was truly ready to share the extraordinary journey Frankie and I had taken. I knew I had given the memoir my all. It was now time to stand proud and let my light shine. It was also time to repay Frankie for all the blessings she had brought to my life.

It was because of Frankie that I had gained a newfound confidence. I now owned my authenticity more than ever before and was living a life filled with what mattered to me.

Still, I found myself stressed in the days leading up to the big event. I had no idea how many people to expect for my book launch, and at times crazy thoughts would run through my mind, like, *What if no one shows up? What if no one cares about my story? Who do you think you are to have written a book?* And the hardest one of all: *What if I look like a fool?*

Thankfully, I knew from reading and hearing about other authors' experiences—as well as having launched two children's books in 2008 and 2010—that everything I was feeling and thinking was normal. I just had to push past the fear. I was confident I could. When fear did rear its ugly head, it helped to remember the motto I had shared with thousands of children and adults when doing my presentations with Frankie: Always be positive, make a difference, and keep on rolling!

Lastly, I reminded myself that the book and its launch was my way of repaying all that Frankie had done for me. There was no way I was going to let her down.

The morning of my book launch, I—along with my sister Paula—went to the Art Center to prepare the space. While we were arranging the tables and chairs, a woman from the florist across the street stopped in with a bouquet of flowers. When I read the card and saw they were from Donna and Jackie, two of the ladies that were in *The Artist's Way* workshop with me—I was truly touched.

With Paula's help, I was finished and home within the hour. I worked on a few projects and then tried to take a nap. I hadn't slept well the night before because of the anticipation of the festivities, and although I was tired, sleep eluded me once again.

Finally I got up and decided to give Joie a bath. I gently placed her in the kitchen sink and allowed the shampoo and warm water to cascade over her tiny body. After rinsing her off,

I dried her with a fluffy bath towel, wrapped her in a blanket and carried her to the sofa.

"You know, Joie," I said quietly, "tonight is a big night for you and me. You are going to meet many new friends." Her jet black eyes looked adoringly into mine, melting my heart. "Papa will be there with you and I'll be nearby too, so you don't need to worry, okay?"

She continued to gaze at me intently. I got the sense that she understood what I was saying. Well, at least I hoped she did.

Before I knew it, it was time for me to get ready. The week before I'd gone to Allechant Boutique, a lovely local shop, and bought a new top especially for the occasion. It was long, down to my knees, with slits down each sleeve, and blue and black with a thin thread of sparkly silver running through it. I paired it with black leggings and knee-high black boots. For a finishing touch I added a long blue scarf with the same silver sparkle and fringes on the ends.

Once I was dressed, I grabbed the Hug-a-Dog Harness® I had bought for Joie shortly after I adopted her. As I put it on her, I smiled when I saw that it too had a silver sparkle of thread running through the black and blue paisley pattern. It hadn't been my intention to match, but it was certainly a nice touch.

It was a cold February night, so John ran out a few minutes early and started the car. I had no idea what to expect, but as I picked Joie up, tucked her under my arm, and walked out the front door, I silently reminded myself to breathe, and trust that all would go well. First and foremost, I reminded myself to enjoy the evening and just have fun.

Shortly after John, Joie and I arrived at Plymouth Art Center, we were joined by Paula and my friends Nikki, Victoria and Marie. Each had been assigned a task—handling book sales, taking pictures, or taking care of the refreshment table—to ensure that the event went smoothly.

Nikki was my photographer, charged with snapping shots of the guests as they milled around. Before they arrived she got shots of me next to a stack of my books and with the cake, which was decorated with the front cover. I had used a photo of me and Frankie hanging out on the end of a friend's pier. It was one of my favorites, and the choice of more than five-hundred people who voted on my Facebook page.

As I moved about in the room, making sure everything was ready, I noticed Joie was right on my heels. She was whimpering, and I realized she was having a hard time getting traction on the tile floor. I pulled her orange rubber booties out of my bag and placed them on her front paws. Although she was able to move about better, she continued to whimper. She simply wanted to be wherever I was.

I picked her up and tried to comfort her, but there was no way I could hold her the entire evening. I handed her off to John and was relieved when she settled into his arms, calm and content. Still, her eyes followed me about the room.

Victoria was busy setting up the refreshment table, making a punch of lemonade and white soda and setting out the pretty heart-shaped sugar cookies she had baked for the occasion. Each cookie had either pink or red frosting and a paw print in the center. They were perfect!

The invitations I sent out weeks before stated the party would begin at six-thirty, so I was surprised and pleased when my first guests—my eighty-two-year-old friend Laverne and her companion Floyd—arrived promptly at six. Laverne and I had forged a special connection several years earlier, when she showed up at a pet grief support group I volunteered for. She needed help dealing with the loss of her beloved Dalmatian, and after several months of attending the monthly meetings, she announced she was ready to adopt another. She came to me and my sister-in-law Lori, who also volunteered for the group, for advice on how to get a dog through a rescue organization. All her other Dals had come from breeders.

"I know this will be my last one," she'd said, "so I want it to be a rescue."

This was all Lori and I had to hear. Between the two of us we were able to help lead Laverne to a five-year-old named Suzie. They enjoyed five years together before Suzie got sick. I will never forget the day Laverne called to ask me if I would come to the clinic to help her say goodbye to her beloved friend. I was honored that she had asked me and it was a privilege to now see her at my book launch.

I thanked her for coming, then turned to John, who was standing with Joie a few feet away. "Laverne," I said as I waved him over, "I want you to meet Joie. She is the new little love of my life."

Laverne's hand shook as she reached out to pat Joie on the top of the head. "I still miss Suzie so much," she said, her eyes misting over, "But it was because of you that I had her. I wanted to be here tonight and get your book."

I reached out and gently squeezed her hand. I understood what it was like to lose a beloved dog. "Well, I'm very glad you and Floyd are here." I pointed to the refreshment table. "Now, please, help yourselves to some cake, cookies, and punch. We will be starting soon, so find a spot to sit and relax, okay?"

Laverne smiled, then slipped her arm through Floyd's and they shuffled their way toward the front row. It was really endearing to see them side-by-side, there for each other in this final chapter of their lives. A moment later, Victoria, always the perfect hostess, walked over and offered to bring them some refreshments.

Other guests began to arrive, and before I knew it nearly every chair in the room was full with family and friends. As I watched Nikki happily snapping their pictures, I chuckled to myself and wondered why I had worried so much. Everything was turning out beautifully. Then again, I had yet to give my talk.

When most of the guests were seated, I pulled a chair to the front of the room and set my notes on it. As I glanced out into the audience, the butterflies in my stomach came to life once again. For so many years I had done presentations, but they were mostly for strangers. Tonight I'd be speaking to those closest to me, and for some reason it was even scarier.

Finally, I took a deep breath and raised my right hand high in the air to get everyone's attention. "I think we will get stared now," I said, projecting my voice as loud as I could.

Within moments, the chatter in the room had ceased and all eyes were on me. "Thanks for coming out tonight, everyone. It really means so much to me to see you all here."

I thanked everyone for coming; then because I tend to talk quietly and didn't have a microphone, I asked, "Can everyone hear me okay?"

A moment later, I heard a familiar voice yell, "What?"

The room erupted into laughter, and I looked up to see my dad and his wife, Lil, in one of the last rows. His face split into a grin.

"I should have known you'd be the smarty pants, Dad," I said, grateful to him for breaking the ice.

Then, with another deep breath, I began sharing Frankie's story. For some, it was the first time hearing about how at six-and-a-half-years old this normal, healthy dog had become paralyzed from IVDD.

"Frankie was definitely my heart dog. She taught me so much about life. It's because of her that I'm the person I am today. She never seemed to mind that her back legs didn't work; she was determined to live her life to the fullest, and her wheelchair was just a tool to help her do that. Through her perseverance in the face of adversity, she helped me see that I could live a more meaningful life. She also taught me to not be afraid to be who I am."

Then I repeated my favorite Anais Nin quote: *And the day came when the risk to remain tight in a bud was more painful than the risk to let it blossom.*

I believe this wholeheartedly, and Frankie had been the catalyst for me to bloom. It never ceased to amaze me that I learned some of life's greatest lessons from a dog that was only ten inches high, shaped like a hot dog and rolled around in a wheelchair.

I remember one particular day about a year after her diagnosis. We were hanging out in the backyard, and I had taken her out of her wheelchair so she could roll around in the grass and white clover. As she wiggled about on her back, I smiled, taking delight in the fact that she was so happy.

Suddenly it occurred to me that even through everything she had been through the past few months, she never once felt sorry for herself, even though she was now paralyzed. It was another lesson I let sink into my heart.

I realized that I was being presented with a beautiful opportunity—using Frankie's fortitude as an example, I could help others facing challenges to deal with them in a positive way. This is what led me to write the two children's books and visit schools, hospitals and nursing homes.

One lesson I especially loved sharing with children was that even though Frankie was in a wheelchair she was *still Frankie*. Her body may look and work a little differently, but her mind and spirit remained the same. Even as I taught this to others, I was learning to let go of the guilt and shame I had been carrying for so long. And as a result, I was beginning to unfold and bloom, just like the bud in the Anais Nin quote. Finally, I shared with the audience the first review of my book, which I had received just a few weeks earlier. "At first glance Techel's story may seem to lack drama—she is an ordinary person, a middle-aged wife, and dog owner in search of a satisfying career, a sense of purpose, an authentic life. Yet, this is exactly the book's appeal. Techel's search is shared by all of us regardless of our circumstances and thus, her story becomes our own."

At first, I had taken it as a negative, that I and my book were lackluster. But then I realized that the reviewer was actually paying me a compliment: we all face similar challenges and oftentimes keep them buried. In sharing my story, I was encouraging people to face what was holding them back and live fully, from the center of who they are, just as Frankie had done for me.

Afterward, I read an excerpt from the book. It was the story of a little boy named Jackson who has a form of cerebral palsy. Jackson and his family came into my life after reading my first children's book, *Frankie the Walk 'N Roll Dog.*

Jackson connected with Frankie because just as she'd had to accept using a wheelchair, he had to wear a new brace on his leg at night. According to his mother he had resisted wearing it. But reading about Frankie helped him adjust.

"I'm just like Frankie," he'd said.

I found myself choking up as I shared Jackson's story, and when I looked up at the audience I noticed many people had tears in their eyes, too.

For those who had not heard the news, I mentioned Frankie's passing the previous June and said that while I had grieved deeply for her, I believed we had been brought together for a divine purpose. "I truly believe she came here with a special mission. She chose me to help her to achieve it and I'll always be so honored to have been her partner. She did her work so gracefully, touching many lives, and ultimately helped me heal in ways I never imagined."

Holding my hands together in prayer in front of my heart, I bowed slightly and said "thank you" to indicate I was finished with my talk.

A welcoming applause broke out. It felt like a warm, loving embrace and made me feel so incredibly good.

After the applause died down, I introduced Joie. I shared with everyone how I had come to adopt her and that she had the same disc disease as Frankie. "Many people have asked me if Joie will do the same work as Frankie did, visiting schools and doing therapy dog work. I don't know yet if she will be up for that. We do have a school visit scheduled in May and I'll see how that goes. But no matter what, she is carrying on Frankie's legacy with stories and photos I share of her on my blog and Facebook. And for that I am grateful."

Now, as I recall saying those words, I realize that I was feeling this pressure to continue the same work I'd done with Frankie. At the time, it felt like an outside force, but I eventually realized that most of it was my own internal struggle. Eventually that inner voice would continue to get louder until I could no longer ignore it.

In many ways, the evening of my book launch felt like I had come full circle. While I was still uncertain about my future, I knew that I was now strong enough to stand on my own. Frankie had given me that gift. Only time would tell how my life with Joie would play out.

CHAPTER ELEVEN

Joie Goes to School

The next three months brought with them a flurry of online promotion and radio interviews. Being so busy made it easier for me to push away that inner nudging that was trying to get my attention.

I knew what I was doing, but yet I wasn't ready to face the fear I had attached to my internal conflict. Every time it tried to get my attention, I'd push it aside. And every time I did my inner self would beat myself up for doing so.

This in turn would have me upset with myself. After everything I'd learned from Frankie, I felt like I'd taken two huge steps backwards. I wasn't willing to address the different issues that were bothering me—all because I was too afraid of the unknown. Even though I was becoming increasingly uncomfortable with these feelings, it was easier to be comfortable in being uncomfortable.

Whether I was on the radio or running into an old friend, it seemed I was asked the same questions: "Was Joie going to be a therapy dog and visit schools?" It got to the point where I'd feel my body clench almost before they even said anything. I knew of course that they didn't mean any harm; I was just having a difficult time letting go of an identity I had tied myself so closely to—even though a part of me wanted to release it.

I had booked one school visit with Joie, a few weeks away. It was essentially the same presentation I had done hundreds of times before, but its main focus had always been Frankie. Now, as I tried to incorporate Joie into it, I found myself struggling, and the ease with which it had come together the first time around seemed to have evaporated. Part of the problem—a part I didn't want to admit even to myself—was that I sometimes compared Joie to Frankie.

Eventually, though, an outline started to come together, and I began to feel excited about sharing this new presentation with young children. I told myself that just maybe this was meant to be. But that thought was immediately followed by a quiet inner voice reminding me that I also wanted more balance in my life.

Still, I kept pushing forward. I told myself I had to *at least* give it a shot. Maybe I would just do fewer school visits than I had with Frankie. This would leave me more time for other projects. For now, the notion helped appease my restless mind.

The day of our school visit was dark, cold and rainy. I forced myself to get out of my warm bed and bent down next to Joie's kennel. As I gently took her out, I silently prayed she was up for our presentation. While I knew she had come from a house of four children, I wasn't sure how she'd be in a room full of very excited kids eager to see a dog in a wheelchair.

Two hours later, I pulled into the parking lot of the small Lutheran school. By now the rain was coming down sideways and the wind had really picked up. Covering my head with the hood of my periwinkle jacket, I jumped out of my car, ran to the back to open the hatch and took out the suitcase with everything I needed for my presentation. Running around to the side of the car, I quickly unbuckled Joie from her car seat, grabbed the handle of my suitcase, and made a mad dash for the front door.

Susan, who had booked me for the visit, was waiting for me inside the door, opening it as I approached. "I'm so sorry you had to come out on such a terrible day!"

I smiled. "No worries. I'm happy to be here."

"Well, the kids and the staff are excited about your visit." A big smile spread across her face as she reached out and patted the top of Joie's head. "We will be in the gym for your presentation."

Susan led me down the dimly lit hall with low ceilings and stopped in front of heavy double doors. My eyes filled with tears when we walked into the gym. I saw that the walls were covered with large handmade posters, all of Frankie. At the front of the room there was a table and a large screen.

I wiped my eyes, then buckled Joie into her wheelchair and spread out a blanket on the floor in case she wanted to rest. Then I quickly set up my laptop with my PowerPoint presentation and set a copy of *Frankie the Walk 'N Roll Dog* on the table provided for me.

Twenty minutes later, kids started filing into the gym. As they did, I took Joie out of her wheelchair and tucked her inside the pink Take-A-Long-Bag™ I'd often carried Frankie in. Especially made for dachshunds, it went around one shoulder and across the front of my stomach.

The room was buzzing with chatter; it echoed off the walls as more and more kids walked in and found spots to sit on the floor. Some shouted, "Joie!" and some even said, "Frankie!"

As soon as everyone was seated, one of the staff members got their attention with a hand signal and asked them to quiet down. The principal then introduced me and Joie and a thunderous applause broke out.

All eyes were on Joie as I started my presentation. "Joie and I are very happy to be here today. Thank you for having us! Before we begin, I just want to say that if you all promise to be very good today then at the end of the presentation you will be able to see Joie walk in her wheelchair and have a chance to pet her."

I'd learned over the years that saying this at the beginning helped keep my audiences quiet and attentive.

My presentation, similar to the one I had done so often with Frankie, shared how we all have challenges and the choice as to how we respond to them. It was always my goal to encourage children to see the positive side in challenges to make it easier to move through them.

After talking for a few moments, I called for a volunteer to come up and help me. As always, just about every hand in the room went up.

It was hard to choose from the sea of sweet, eager, happy faces, all wanting to help. This time I chose a dark-haired little girl sitting in the second row who appeared to be in either first or second grade.

As she walked to the front of the room, I took Joie out of the pink bag, set her on the table and held her in place. With my free hand I motioned for the girl to join me behind the table, all the while praying this would work. Joie could be quite wiggly.

Glancing down at the girl, I said, "Thank you for volunteering. What's your name?"

"Cindy," she said so quietly that I almost didn't hear her.

I explained to Cindy and the audience how Joie's wheelchair opens, and how Cindy was going to help me place Joie in its saddle. Cindy's eyes grew wider as she looked up at me, and she nodded her head yes.

Once the wheelchair was in the open position, I took Cindy's tiny hands in mine and guided them to either side of Joie's belly. "Okay, on the count of three, we will gently pick Joie's back end up and place her back feet through each hole in the saddle. I'll help you."

Cindy nodded her head up and down once again.

"One…two…three!"

As we lifted Joie up, she started to wiggle, making it difficult to get her legs into each side of the saddle opening. It took three more tries before we were finally able to get her fitted properly inside the wheelchair. I carefully hid my frustration—after all—the point was to show the children that having a dog who needs a wheelchair can be a positive experience—and made a mental note to practice this with Joie ahead of future school visits.

"Thank you for helping, Cindy. You did a great job!" Looking out into the audience I said, "Let's give Cindy a round of applause for being a great helper today."

As the children and staff clapped, Cindy returned to her spot on the floor, smiling from ear to ear. I took Joie back out of her wheelchair and placed her in the pink bag still hanging around my shoulder.

Once the clapping died down, I read three pages of *Frankie the Walk 'N Roll Dog* to the kids. Afterwards, I shared photos on the large screen of Frankie and Joie. This was always a hit, and most of the kids giggled or broke out in a chorus of, "Awww!"

It was time for the grand finale, and my favorite moment of the presentation. Watching as the children witnessed a dog walking in a wheelchair—usually for the first time—always filled the room with excitement and made my heart soar.

Frankie and I had gotten this down to a science. She would stand beside me, her eyes riveted to my pants pocket and the treats she knew I had in there. I would take a treat out, show it to Frankie, then throw it a few feet in front of her. With great enthusiasm she'd roll off to fetch the treat, to ooohs, ahhhs and applause from the audience. It always went off without a hitch.

Joie wasn't as treat-orientated, but I still hoped we could pull this off. I had even put Joie's booties on so she'd be able to gain traction on the slippery gym floor.

Kneeling on the floor, I strapped Joie into her wheelchair. "Okay everyone, I need all of you to be very quiet please. Also, please stay seated. This way everyone will be able to see Joie walk in her wheelchair."

The room was so quiet you could have heard a pin drop. All eyes were on Joie as I took a treat out of my pocket, showed it to her, then tossed it a few feet away.

She looked at the treat, but didn't budge. I threw another treat, which landed near the first one. She looked again, but still didn't move. Getting nervous now, I tried once more. Finally, she started to slowly move forward. I watched with delight as she picked up speed, rolling right into the kids sitting in the front row and instantly creating a wave of giggles.

I hoped she would keep walking, but she just wasn't up for it and no amount of treats and sweet talk was going to change that. Not wanting to cause her any undue stress, I took her out of the wheelchair and placed her back inside the pink bag. It had turned out okay, but we still had a lot of work ahead of us.

"Thank you everyone for being such wonderful listeners! We can take a few moments now if anyone has questions." For the next fifteen minutes I answered many questions, which was another favorite part of mine.

Afterwards, Susan walked to the front of room and stood next to me and Joie. "Our school has something we'd like to present you with," she said, then motioned toward three eighth grade students standing nearby.

They came forward and thanked me and Joie for visiting their school, then one of them unfolded and held up a small t-shirt. It was yellow and navy, the school colors, and had the school's name on it. The best part though were all the signatures written in permanent marker. One of the students said, "This is for Joie. Many of us signed the t-shirt for her."

My voice caught a bit as I said, "Thank you for such a beautiful gift. Joie and I will always treasure it." Then, as promised, I told them that since they had been so good during the presentation they would have a chance to pet Joie. Everyone burst out in a loud cheer.

I quickly walked to the gym entrance with Joie still in her pink pouch and waited for the kids to line up. Joie seemed just as pleased to meet them, relishing each soft pat on the head, each scratch under the chin. I even noticed that now and then she would close her eyes as if soaking in all the good energy. I was so proud of her.

Driving home that day, I reflected on how the morning went and decided I felt okay about it. Sure, there was some work to do before we attempted another school presentation, but with summer just around the corner, we wouldn't have to worry about that for a while. Joie and I had plenty of time to practice.

CHAPTER TWELVE

Once in a Lifetime Call

As spring turned to summer, I looked forward to more leisurely days that season always seemed to bring with it. Little did I know my life was about to change again.

For the past year I had been mentoring my young friend, Nikki. Married for three years to her college sweet-heart, she was having second thoughts about staying in the relationship. We had spent countless hours together as she talked through her feelings and carefully weighed both sides; now, as Memorial Day weekend approached, Nikki announced that was as ready as she would ever be to move out of the home she shared with her husband.

I was not surprised by her decision; in fact, from our long conversations it had seemed to me inevitable. I also knew that she would need somewhere inexpensive to live until she got on her feet. Wanting to help in any way I could, I'd talked to John, even before I knew of her final decision.

John had been a bit surprised when I told him that Nikki was about to leave her marriage. While he was aware that she was going through a tough time, he didn't know all the details. He was even more surprised when I added, "I'd really like to offer her our lower level for a while."

Years ago we had fixed up the eleven-hundred square foot space, adding a family room, bedroom and bathroom. We had also planned to add a bar, but chose instead to turn the area with the linoleum floor into a small kitchen. John, being a carpenter by trade, was easily able to add a few cabinets and a sink.

Surprised or not, he didn't hesitate to help. "I think that's a great idea." He had grown as fond of Nikki as I was and enjoyed when she came over.

That's not to say it wouldn't be an adjustment. John and I never had children, and are for the most part private people—not the sort to casually ask someone to share our home. But given our special bond with Nikki and after thoroughly talking things over, we decided it felt right. Plus, I was still wrestling with what I wanted to tackle next; maybe this was where I needed to be right now, helping to support a distraught young woman.

Once we made the decision, everything fell into place. Nikki moved in at the end of May and quickly made the lower level her own. It was so quaint and cozy that I often joked that I was going to move in myself.

When offering her the space I'd told Nikki that she should treat it like a separate apartment, as if John and I weren't right upstairs. Setting boundaries was important to me. But little by little she began to ease into our everyday life.

On the weekends, John and I liked to sit at the kitchen table, him with his cup of coffee and me with my tea. We'd talk about the events of the past week and what we had planned for the day. I cherished those quiet times with him. But before long Nikki began to come upstairs, peek her head in the doorway and ask if she could join us.

While I didn't mind, exactly, there was a part of me that struggled with having her intertwined in our daily life. I was used to having a lot of time by myself, or with John and the dogs, and now that seemed to be happening less and less. When I told John how I felt, he said Nikki just needed to be around people. He was probably right, I told myself, and besides, this was only temporary. I just had to be patient.

Although I continued to experience mixed emotions about Nikki staying with us, I never said anything to her about it or discouraged her from coming around. I began to see what a blessing it was to have her there, sharing in our lives.

Nikki was with me one day in early June when I received a phone call from Angela of the Wisconsin Humane Society. I exchanged pleasantries with her for a few minutes, all the while wondering about the reason for the call. Finally, she got down to business.

"Barb, I'm calling because I received a call from a producer who will be filming a movie in our area later this summer."

"Wow, that is exciting!" I said, still unsure what that had to do with me.

"He is looking for a dog in a wheelchair to play a small part in the film, and of course I thought of you. I know Frankie passed away but I thought you might know of someone else who has a dog in a wheelchair."

Grinning from ear to ear, I said, "Well, actually I do happen to know of someone…"

"You do? That is wonderful," she said. "Are they from the area? The producer would really like someone local."

"Yes, you could say that," I said, then paused for a moment. "It's me and my new little dog, Joie!"

"You have another dog in a wheelchair?"

"Yup! I adopted her last October from Oregon Dachshund Rescue. She is black and tan and has the same disc disease like Frankie did."

"Oh, bless your heart for taking in another special needs dog."

"Thanks, but it's really all because of Frankie. If it wasn't for her I never would have considered a special needs pet."

"That really is wonderful, Barb," she said. "The producer's name is Jeff Gendelman, and he asked that if I found someone to have them call him directly. He will give you the details."

"Okay, sure." I grabbed a piece of paper and pencil. "What's his number?"

My hands were shaking a little as Angela read off Jeff's number to me. This was so exciting, and a bit nerve-wracking as well.

"Thanks so much, Angela. I will call him right away."

"Good luck, Barb, and keep me posted!"

After I hung up the phone I just sat there for a few moments, not quite able to believe I was being given this wonderful opportunity. I reminded myself that no matter how great the idea sounded, I was not going to subject Joie to anything too stressful. The conditions had to be right, if she was even a good fit for the project.

My hands were shaking again as I picked up my cell and punched in Jeff's number. He picked up on the third ring.

"Hi Barbara," he said when I explained who I was and why I was calling, "Angela told me about you and said you might know of someone else in the area who has a dog in a wheelchair."

Smiling once again, I explained that I had adopted another dachshund with disc disease and adjusted Frankie's wheelchair to fit her.

"That's great! Well, let me tell you a little about the film. It's called *The Surface,* and we will begin shooting in late August in the Bayshore area. The movie is based on a true story and takes place on Lake Michigan. There is a family scene where one of the main characters has a flashback. The character is based on a good friend of mine who had a dog in a wheelchair, though his dog was a German shepherd.

"I see," I said.

"Do you by chance know of anyone who has a larger dog in a wheelchair?"

Swallowing my disappointment that Joie was not what he was looking for I said, "Well, not off the top of my head. I can certainly put the word out to my network to see if I can't find someone for you. I did know of a German shepherd in the Milwaukee area, but she has since passed away."

Jeff paused a moment. "Okay, tell you what. Why don't you email me a few pictures of Joie. The director is coming to town in early July and I will talk to him and see what he thinks."

"I'd be happy to send you some pictures, Jeff, but can you tell me a bit more about what the part will require? I just want to make sure it's not too much for Joie."

"Oh, of course," Jeff said. He went on to tell me that the scene would be filmed inside a home located in Mequon. Joie would only have to walk down the hallway where she would be greeted by the daughter of one of the main characters. It would probably only take a couple of hours.

"That sounds easy enough. I think Joie could do that."

"Great. Well, like I said, the director will be here in early July. I will find out how he feels about Joie playing the part. I can't make any promises, but as soon as he makes a decision I'll let you know."

"Sounds good."

"So if this works out, would you and Joie be available the last two weeks of August?"

"Yes, I can make that happen."

"Wonderful. Also, there isn't any compensation as this is a low budget film. But it will be a wonderful opportunity."

"I understand, and I agree that it is a great opportunity. I really appreciate it." I was about to say goodbye when suddenly I found myself telling him about the work I'd done with Frankie and the day I founded in her memory, National Walk 'N Roll Dog Day.

"That's really great," he said, "Perhaps we can include that in the closing credits."

I was more excited about that than the thought of a paycheck. Thanking him again, I promised to send the pictures of Joie right away.

After we ended the call, I bent down to Joie, who was lying in her bed at my feet, and picked her up. "Can you believe it, Joie?" I said as I held her in my lap, "You might be in a movie! Wouldn't that be awesome?"

She just stared back at me, oblivious to this once-in-a-lifetime opportunity. Hugging her close, I then went out to the yard to share the news with Nikki.

An aspiring artist, she liked to spread a blanket under our large locust tree and see what inspired her.

Sure enough, she was sitting beneath the tree, crossed-legged. Her face was partially hidden by the wide-brim green and white striped straw hat she wore, but I could see she was totally lost in sketching a scene of people on a beach. It brought a smile to my face.

Nikki heard my footsteps and turned to look at me.

"Hey Nikki! I've got some exciting news!"

Setting down her pencil, she said, "Really? What is it?"

"Joie might be in a movie!"

"Wow, that *is* exciting! How did that happen?"

Nikki smiled as I filled her in on the details. She knew I had been struggling to find my way again after Frankie died and agreed that the movie would be an amazing opportunity to show people how special needs dogs could live quality lives.

"That's awesome, Barb," Nikki said, "I hope it works out."

I glanced at Joie as she sniffed around in the grass, oblivious to the fact that she might soon be a movie star. "Well, if it is meant to be, it will happen."

Later that day when John came home from work I shared the news with him, too. As always, he was excited for me and Joie. It was another reminder how blessed I am for his steadfast support.

Now the waiting game began. All I could do now was try not to think about it. As with all lessons on patience, it would be easier said than done.

CHAPTER THIRTEEN

Deepening Our Bond

The next morning was the first Saturday of June and the official opening of the local Farmers and Artisans market. Each year, I looked forward to the market, for it had become an enjoyable weekly social outing and a break from the solitude of my writing cottage. I even had my own booth from which I sold my books, and many of the regulars would come to visit with me and Frankie. I planned on having the booth again this year and hoped Joie would be willing to hang out.

When I woke up the sun was shining and a check of the forecast confirmed that it would be in the low 70s—perfect market weather. I quickly dressed and found Nikki already waiting for me in the kitchen. I had asked her the night before if she wanted to come along, an offer she eagerly accepted. I just hoped Joie would be as excited about it.

After my nerve-wracking experience with Joie at the massage class, I knew I had to find a way to socialize her. I thought perhaps if I exposed her to other dogs in an environment I felt comfortable with, then hopefully she would become comfortable too. Nikki and I arrived at the market around ten a.m. We started out by walking the perimeter, past many vendors in the white pop-up canopies hawking their products and produce. Joie walked beside me in her wheelchair, and many people stopped to ask about her.

A few moments later, her first encounter with a small, white dog did not go well. The minute she laid eyes on the dog she started to bark frantically, so much so that people stopped what they were doing and looked to see what was going on. It sounded as though she was being attacked.

I scooped her up in my arms and turned her away from the dog. When that didn't work, I tried to distract her with a treat, but she was having nothing to do with it. She wanted to know where the dog was and she was fighting me with everything she had.

Thankfully, I had brought the pink pouch that Joie seemed to feel so safe in. I put it around my shoulder and tucked her inside, carrying her wheelchair in my hand. I'd hoped this would make her feel more secure so Nikki and I could shop the market.

At first Joie was content to be in the bag, but every time she saw, or even sensed a dog nearby, she became visibly upset. As for me, I was both frustrated and sad to see her in such distress.

On our final encounter with yet another dog, Joie had an accident and pooped in the pink pouch. I turned to Nikki and said, "We need to head home."

Nikki was a good sport about it, but she was probably disappointed that we were leaving the market early. I know I was. I fought my annoyance on the way to the house. As I gave Joie a bath in the sink I questioned who I was more annoyed with—Joie or myself. I was well aware that dogs sense our emotions—perhaps Joie had picked up on my uneasiness about what would happen when we encountered other dogs.

I wanted so badly to help Joie feel safe, happy and secure, but how? That's when I got the idea to reach out to my friend Dawn. A knowledgeable animal communicator, she provided me with comforting insight when I was getting ready to say goodbye to Frankie. Maybe she could help me with Joie as well.

Two days later, Dawn and I were talking by phone. I had already sent her a few pictures of Joie, which she would use during the reading to get in tune with her energy and try to determine the core issues around her reaction to other dogs. When I shared my concerns with Dawn, she said, "I feel like Joie may have had some trauma from when she was younger, along with some emotional issues that seem to be lodged."

"Do you think the trauma is related to her paralysis?"

She paused for a moment. "I'm not sure," she said. "Joie is showing me that the plane ride she took to fly to you was traumatic for her. She's also still adjusting to you, John and Kylie."

"That makes sense."

"She isn't quite sure how to be a dog. She is sharing with me that she feels nervous at times. She wants to feel more grounded."

Hearing this, my heart ached. "What can I do to help her?"

"Well, one thing I'd suggest is more silly play time with her. This will help establish a connection between you. Also, meditation may be good, and perhaps at some point inviting Frankie into the meditation."

"Okay," I said, feeling a bit better, "I can do these things."

"Hang on a moment. Joie is trying to share something else." Dawn was silent for a few moments before she spoke again.

"Ah, yes. Joie just shared with me that she knows you are still holding onto Frankie."

Hot tears instantly spray to my eyes and my throat tightened. It was true; although I had made some progress moving through the loss of Frankie, I was still trying to hold onto what *was*. It was difficult to hear, yet I also felt a sense of relief.

"She's right, Dawn," I said finally.

I could hear the tenderness in her voice as she said, "Things with you and Joie have to evolve organically. You can't force it."

"I know." And I did understand I couldn't force Joie to be something she wasn't. She was never going to be Frankie, nor did I want her to. I was also well aware that I was not going to be the same person as I had been with Frankie, and of my own internal struggle to move forward in a new way.

As my session with Dawn drew to a close, I thanked her for her help and promised to keep her posted about my progress with Joie. I also thanked Joie for speaking to me through Dawn so that she and I might grow closer. I ended the call and sat there for a few moments, just thinking about all I had learned.

Suddenly it occurred to me that perhaps Reiki would be beneficial for Joie. I had become attuned a few years before but hadn't really practiced, due in part to a lack of confidence around it. Now, however, I was wondering whether I should take it up in earnest.

The next morning I awoke eager to begin a new day with Joie. A while back I had bought Kathleen Prasad's *Reiki for Dogs* but hadn't had much time to read it. Now, as I took it from my book shelf and began skimming some of the chapters, I realized Joie was about to teach me some new things.

According to Reiki.org, *Reiki is a Japanese technique for stress reduction and relaxation that also promotes healing. It is administered by "laying on hands" and is based on the idea that an unseen "life force energy" flows through us and is what causes us to be alive. If one's life force energy is low, then we are more likely to get sick or feel stress, and if it is high, we are more capable of being happy and healthy.*

According to Prasad, however, the "laying on of hands" may not be suitable for dogs. She encourages pet owners to refrain from forcing physical contact and rather hold a space of healing for the pet.

"By simply relaxing, being quiet, breathing, and having a heartfelt intention to help another being, you can create a sacred space," she wrote. "In this space, all things are possible. You simply allow the energy to flow in through your body and out toward the animal."

She suggested starting with thirty to sixty-minute sessions for four days in a row. I didn't know how I was going to sit still for that amount of time, but if it meant helping Joie I was up for the challenge. Besides, for the past twelve years my dogs had been some of my greatest teachers. Clearly there was more to be done, and I was curious to see how Reiki could improve our relationship.

Later that afternoon, Joie and I had our first Reiki session. Before beginning, I mentally searched the house for the quietest spot. I decided it was in my bedroom closet. John and Nikki were often in and out and I didn't want to be disturbed once I got into a sacred, quiet space with Joie.

"Come on, Joie," I called. "Let's go chill out for a little while."

She had been lying in her wheelchair on her bed in the kitchen, but now she got up and followed me right into the closet.

I closed the door, rolled out my yoga mat, and sat cross-legged on it. Before I closed my eyes, I glanced at Joie and noted that she had laid down just a few feet from me. I sensed she was content. As much as I wanted her to sit closer to me, I recalled Kathleen Prasad's advice to just let your dog approach you if he or she wished.

I took a few deep breaths and slowly closed my eyes, trying to center myself and clear my mind. It was not easy. I wondered how in the world I was going to sit still for an entire half hour! It felt like an eternity, and the more I told myself to settle down the more restless I became.

But it was important to tap into the Japanese energy centers that is Reiki. As stated in Prasad's book, "According to

Japanese philosophy, as taught by Frans and Bronwen Stiene of International House of Reiki, there are three energy centers in the body: the *hara* (below the navel), which connects you with earth energy; the *middle hara* (found at your heart), which connects you with your human experience; and the *upper hara* (found in your head), which connects you with heaven energy."

I reminded myself I wanted to do this for Joie. It was important to me to do what I could to help her feel more at ease.

Taking in a few more deep breaths, I concentrated on tapping into the energy of earth and how important it is to set this foundation first so that a space of harmony, peace and courage can open. I did this by imagining I had roots like a tree growing out the bottom of my feet and reaching down into the earth. This helped ground me.

Next, I allowed the healing energy of the universe to flow through me. Silently, I invited Joie to take whatever she needed for her own healing. I didn't know how much time passed when I felt the need to open my eyes and peek at how Joie was doing. But I didn't judge it and instead honored what I was feeling called to do.

When I looked over at her, I saw she was still lying in the same spot with her eyes on me. But then she closed her eyes. I sensed she was feeling peaceful. Observing Joie in a relaxed state for the remaining time was the boost of confidence I needed to look forward to another session the following day.

The next afternoon, Joie and I were back in the closet. It did feel rather silly to be hanging out in there, but it was better than being interrupted. Fortunately, we have a nice-sized walkin, so it wasn't like I was sitting on top of shoes or purses, nor were we confined in any way.

As I sat on my yoga mat, I noticed that Joie was lying in the same spot as the day before. Closing my eyes, I took a few deep breaths, imagining again roots on the bottom of my feet, reaching down into the earth to ground myself.

I don't know how much time had passed when I heard Joie's wheels rolling toward me. Was she going to sit by me? I welcomed the thought. Sensing that she was nearby, I opened my eyes and found her standing in front of me. I smiled.

She rested her head on my knee as her back end laid down on the floor. My heart melted. What a sweet and pure connection we were having.

Remembering Prasad's words, I tuned into my intuition and let it be my guide. I felt called to place one hand gently on Joie's upper back, and the other on the lower portion of her back. She stayed right where she was and accepted the placement of my hands on her.

I practiced holding a sacred and safe space for Joie, silently running the thought through my mind: *Whatever healing you need, Joie, I offer this space for you to take it in.*

I didn't know for sure if the sessions were helping her, but I decided to trust in the process. Practicing Reiki with Joie was helping me to hand everything over to the divine and have faith that it was helping in some shape or form.

When we returned to the closet on the third day, I once again grounded myself so energy from the earth and heaven could easily flow through me. This time though, I felt called to keep my eyes open. I wanted to observe Joie for a few minutes.

She seemed to inhale deeply a few times, then let them out. I found this rather intriguing being this was the same thing I had been doing each time. Her eyes open, she would close them periodically for just a few seconds before opening them again.

As I sat in this place of stillness with Joie, I remembered that Dawn had suggested asking Frankie if she would join me and Joie during a session.

My spiritual connection with Frankie had been very strong, so much so that she appeared to me as a hummingbird after she passed away. Still, I was a little skeptical that I could call upon her now. Would she really come to me and Joie if I asked? Since embarking on a spiritual path years ago, I was definitely open to giving it a try. I had learned I am part of this universe—a universe that offers us magnificent insight if we allow ourselves to just trust in what we can't see.

I closed my eyes and silently said, *Frankie, are you there? I'd love for you to join me and Joie today if you are up for it.*

A few moments passed and nothing happened. Doubt tried to take over, but I would just as quickly dismiss it. After a few more deep breaths I started to see a white light in my mind's eye. Joie was there too; I saw a light start at the top of her head, then slowly travel down her back and to the tip of her tail. It then traveled back up her body.

Just as the light came to the top of Joie's head, Frankie appeared to me in this space of consciousness within my mind. She was in her wheelchair, which surprised me; I'd thought that once on the other side she would be free of it. But I let the thought go. I didn't want to judge it. I also wanted to truly be in the moment of what was transpiring.

As I write this today, I realize this may sound really "out there." Perhaps some may question my sanity. But to me it *was* real, as was the indescribable feeling of peace, joy and comfort that came over me. I *knew* Frankie was there with us! I saw Frankie put her snout up against Joie's as if greeting her. I was aware of my body, but at the same time I felt like I was floating above it all and bathed in a warm pool of pure love.

Tears were running down my face, but they weren't tears of sadness. They came from the understanding that what was happening in this space was real. They were tears of recognition which helped me to know that we are all connected, whether we're in physical or spiritual form.

Silently I asked: *Hey Frankie, how are you?*

In response, she lay down next to Joie, and I felt this intense joy and deep compassion. I sensed that Frankie was comforting Joie, letting her know everything was going to be okay. This, in turn, gave me a profound sense of peace and comfort.

What I was witnessing and experiencing was so profound, I didn't want it to end. What a gift it was to be with both Joie and Frankie, connected by this magnificent flow of love.

In those precious moments, it was as if we were all suspended in a cloud, with no concept of time. I felt a tremendous shift, as if a weight had been lifted from me. Then, all too soon, I saw Frankie stand up and sensed she was ready to move on once again.

While I didn't want her to go, I realized that Frankie would always be a part of me. I knew now that anytime I wanted to feel her with me, all I had to do is rest within this space of connected consciousness.

Thank you, Frankie. Thank you. I love you so much, I silently said. And just as she had appeared before me a few moments ago, she disappeared.

I took a deep breath, wanting to linger in this sacred space for just a bit longer. Deeply grateful for what I had just experienced, I thanked Joie and closed the Reiki session. Sliding over to Joie, I took her tiny face in my hands.

"I really love you, Joie. We are going to be fine. Yup, we are going to be just fine."

CHAPTER FOURTEEN

A Pivotal Milestone

After that miraculous day, there was definitely a positive shift in my relationship with Joie. We continued our Reiki sessions on an "as-needed" basis, but I understood more clearly now that I had to allow our partnership to unfold in a natural way.

It also became obvious that for the rest of the summer it was my job to just be open to what may be next for me. While I still had many moments of wondering what my purpose was moving forward, I was better able to accept that the next steps would present themselves in due time.

I also had a big milestone around the corner. I was turning fifty in a few weeks. Where had the time gone? I certainly didn't *feel* older. Then again, how was fifty *supposed* to feel?

I am blessed to live in a time where attitudes about aging are shifting in a more positive direction. I certainly strived to keep a confident attitude and not let age dictate how I should live, and indeed, in some ways I felt like my life was truly beginning.

Back in my twenties and thirties I had felt pressure to conform to society's dictates about how we should look. But over the years I had decided it was something I no longer wanted to buy into. Although I sometimes balked when I saw new wrinkles popping up or noticed gravity taking its toll, I was generally more comfortable in my own skin. I welcomed being in this peaceful place of acceptance.

I wasn't the only one having a big birthday; Joie had just turned five in March. It made me wonder, if I could speak to my five-year-old self today, what would I tell her? The question—and my answers—inspired me to write a blog post.

I'd first tell my five-year-old self that I love her and that she is beautiful. I'd tell her I see a light in her heart that shines brightly and to never let anyone dim that light.

I'd tell her to be brave. Be strong. Love yourself first and the rest will follow as it is meant to be.

I'd tell her that her heart will break, but that when it does, joy will return again. You can't experience one without the other.

Boys will tease you, but it's because they like you (I wish I had known this in kindergarten, when a little boy named Mark pulled my pigtails on the playground).

I'd tell her that life isn't always going to be fair, but that she would always have a choice about her attitude.

I'd tell her that wisdom will be shared with her through the great teachings of Dog.

I'd tell her that she will feel odd and left out at times, but to stand tall in who she is—to own her authenticity—to never play small.

I'd tell her to always pay attention to what her heart is whispering, and to not let the loud noises of society drown out those whispers.

I'd tell her to always live from the inside out.

Lastly, I'd tell her that she is safe and loved, and that she always would be.

While I wished I could have known all of this sooner, I was thankful that I had come to these realizations and was continually making positive changes in my life when many others still have fear of doing so. While I still had negative feelings and inner conflict, I was now able to process them in a healthier way.

I didn't want a big birthday bash, and there was no diamond trinket I had my eye on. When it came to my fiftieth I had decided to let the universe surprise me, and boy, did it ever. About two weeks before my birthday, I got a phone call from Jeff Gendelman, the movie producer I had spoken to at the beginning of the summer. He called to let me know that director, Gil Cates, Jr. approved of Joie being in the movie! I was to have her on set on August 19. Jeff said we should arrive by seven a.m., several hours before our scene would be shot.

I was ecstatic. Somehow, having Joie in the movie felt like a whole new beginning for both of us.

On the morning of my birthday I was awake by six. It was about an hour earlier than usual, but I wanted to see John for my birthday kiss before he headed out to a jobsite.

After taking Joie to the bathroom to express her bladder, I headed for the kitchen. Kylie greeted me with a soft head butt to my leg, but John wasn't there. I peeked into his office but found it empty. *Oh well,* I thought, slightly disappointed, *he must have already left for the site.*

I returned to the kitchen, sat down at the table and reached for my iPad, thinking I'd check my emails and Facebook.

A few minutes later I was startled by the sound of voices coming from the garage. The voices grew closer, then John and Nikki walked in through the garage door, grinning like two Cheshire cats.

"Happy Birthday!" Nikki said as she stepped forward to give me a hug.

I glanced past her shoulder at John, who still had a goofy grin on his face. As soon as she released me, he stepped forward and put his arms around me.

"Okay, what have you two been up to?"

"Did you see what we were doing?" Nikki asked.

"What do you mean?"

John and Nikki looked at each other, then burst out giggling like two little kids. "C'mon, let's just take a little walk out onto the deck," she said, already moving toward the door.

Although I had no idea what was going on, their mood was infectious. Smiling, I picked up Joie and tucked her under my right arm, then followed them out to the deck. My smile grew broader as I glanced over at my writing cottage and saw that the door was decorated with pink balloons and streamers. There was also sign on the door that read, "Happy 50th Birthday, Barb!"

"So this is what you two have been up to!"

"But oh, there is more!" Nikki said.

She walked toward the cottage and opened the door, motioning for me to enter. I gasped when I walked inside and saw what John and Nikki had done for my special day.

Every of inch of the ten by twelve space was covered with colorful streamers and balloons. The centerpiece was a long Happy Birthday banner that ran from one end of the room to the other.

"Thank you so much," I said, deeply moved. "This is so sweet."

"But wait! There is more!" Nikki said again, then she reached behind me and grabbed something off of the desk. After a pause for effect, she held out her hands and presented me with a silver and pink princess tiara. Placing it upon my head she said, "You are the birthday princess today!"

I laughed. "A tiara on my birthday—this is certainly a first." I squeezed her hand, then turned to John. "Thank you again, both of you. What a great way to start my day."

John still had that grin on his face. "We have one more surprise."

He looked at Nikki and she joyfully shouted, "Cupcakes for breakfast!"

"Perfect," I said. "What else would a girl want for her fiftieth birthday breakfast?"

We all walked back into the house and sat down to a breakfast of cream-filled vanilla cupcakes.

"We dubbed ourselves the 'birthday bandits,'" Nikki said, smiling over her coffee cup. They had gotten up extra early so they could decorate the cottage in time. It was better than any gift I could have thought of, aside from the call from the movie producer, of course.

After our sugary feast, John kissed me and left for work. Nikki also had a full day planned at her studio and headed downstairs to change. They would both be back that evening to take me out to dinner.

The rest of my day was quiet and uneventful, which was fine with me. The gifts I had received—the call from the movie producer and the work of my "birthday bandits"—were better than any gifts I could have thought up.

CHAPTER FIFTEEN

Lights! Camera! Action!

The rest of July flew by quickly, which it always seems to do, I think in part, because aside from October it is my favorite month. That year, I didn't mind, though, because I was looking forward to the day of Joie's screen debut.

Finally, August 19 arrived. After a fitful sleep, I awoke around dawn and began getting ready, hoping my excitement would get me through the long day. Truth be told, I was also a bit concerned that the experience might be too stressful for Joie. I said a silent prayer that the shoot would go smoothly. So far, so good, I thought as she gobbled her breakfast with gusto, oblivious to my anxiety. I, on the other hand, had no appetite and threw a granola bar in my purse in case I got hungry later on.

After she finished eating, I dressed her in her blue paisley harness, grabbed the bag I'd packed the night before with her pink blanket, her favorite blue and pink stuffed toy bone, some treats and her water bowl, and slung it over my shoulder. I had also left her wheelchair by the door so I wouldn't forget it; I grabbed it now, then finally tucked Joie under my right arm and headed out to the car.

It was a forty-five minute drive to Mequon, where the filming was to take place, but I left myself well over an hour. I wanted to beat the rush hour traffic, which can be heavy when heading to that area of the state. I also wanted to be sure I found the house okay and left a cushion in my timing for a wrong turn or two.

Fortunately, the traffic was light at that hour. With one less thing to worry about, my thoughts turned to the media coverage that had been done in our area about the film. It was an unusual movie in that most of the scenes were being shot on the waters of Lake Michigan. I also thought about how excited Jeff must be; apparently, the film had been a dream of his, eighteen years in the making. Now it was finally coming true, and in his own hometown to boot. He was probably on cloud nine.

Before I knew it I had reached the suburb of Bayshore, then the street where the home we were shooting in was located. The place was jammed, with cars lined up almost all the way to the intersection, and a man was standing in the street holding a walkie-talkie. Realizing I wasn't going to get any closer, I took the first available parking spot.

I unbuckled Joie from her car seat and got out of the car. When the man saw me he smiled and walked over.

"Hi! My name is Barbara Techel and this is my dog, Joie. We are expected on set today." Even as the words came out of my mouth, I couldn't quite believe I was saying them. Talk about surreal!

"Great. I'll radio ahead and let them know you are on your way."

"How far down is the house?"

"Less than five minutes," he replied. "A gentleman named Matt will be waiting for you on the other end to escort you inside."

"Okay, thanks!"

I grabbed my purse and bag out of the back seat of the car before walking down the road. A few minutes later I came to a cul-de-sac and was greeted by a young, handsome man with jet-black hair and deep blue eyes.

"You must be Barbara and this must be Joie," he said as he patted the top of Joie's head.

"We sure are."

"I'm Matt. I'll show you where you can hang out until they are ready for your scene."

"Thank you," I said, as I followed him past the front of the home and up the driveway. Big lights and camera equipment were set up on the lawn near the front door, and I wondered what scene they were being used for. It was all so exciting.

There were other people—perhaps extras or part of the crew—standing around with steaming coffees and plates full of food.

Matt led me to the garage, where there were tables set up with bagels, fruit, cereal, and juice; there was even a young man frying eggs.

"Hey everyone," Matt said, "this is Barbara and her dog, Joie. They will be on set today."

Many of the crew members gave us a shout out, some thanking me for bringing Joie, and others remarking on how cute she was. One gentleman thanked me for being part of the film.

"Oh, of course!" I said. "It's really an honor."

Matt pointed to the tables of food. "Feel free to help yourself."

"Thank you. I may do that later." My stomach churned at the sight of food. I was still too nervous to eat.

Matt ushered us through the back door into a large kitchen. In the center was a large, butcher block table with ten or so more people gathered around it. I could see others running around between the dining and living rooms. The place was a hive of activity.

One man looked familiar, and I realized it was Jeff; I had looked him up on Facebook after the second phone call. We made eye contact and he immediately began walking toward me, holding out his hand to shake mine.

"Hi Barbara! Thanks so much for being here today."

"Thank you for asking us to be a part of this," I said. "It's so exciting!"

"We won't be filming Joie's scene for a while yet. Make yourself comfortable in the kitchen."

"Okay," I said as I set my purse and bag down on the table. I realized then that many of the people standing around were looking at Joie and smiling.

A young girl with long, brown hair approached me. Next to her stood a woman who looked to be in her late thirties.

"Barbara, I'd like you to meet my wife Ginny and my daughter, Megan."

"It's so nice to meet you both," I said.

"Joie is so adorable!" Megan exclaimed. "May I pet her?"

"Sure, of course."

"My daughter will be in the scene with Joie," Jeff explained, "She is playing the daughter of one of the main characters, who will also be in the scene."

Glancing at his daughter, he said, "Megan, I'd like you to spend some time with Joie. Play with her and offer her some of the treats we brought along, if that is okay with Barbara."

I nodded in agreement.

"Ask Barbara about the best way to pick Joie up and hold her since you will have to do that in the scene. You might also want to understand how to take Joie out of her wheelchair in case Cates wants you to do that."

Megan nodded and smiled at Joie.

"Okay, great. I'll let you all get to know each other. Let me know if you have any questions or concerns."

"Sure, no problem," I said.

Jeff walked back to the living room where I could see a small crew and cameras set up, and I turned to Megan. As we chatted, I found myself impressed with how professional and sweet she was.

After a few moments, Ginny said, "Okay, Megan, you better practice. You have those treats for Joie, right?"

"Oh yes!" she said as she began looking through her bag. After she had the treats in her hand, we moved to a corner of the kitchen where we wouldn't be in the way and sat down on the tile floor.

From where we sat I could see into the small dining room, where other members of the film crew had gathered. They had copies of the script in hand and were surrounded by cameras, lighting, and screens. It really was thrilling to be on the set of a film!

As Megan played with Joie, softly talking to her, I asked how old she was.

"Twelve," she said.

"This must be exciting for you to play a part in your dad's film."

She shook her head eagerly. "Oh yes, it is! He has been wanting to make this movie for a long time."

"Do you want to be an actress someday or are you doing it to help him out?"

"I really want to be an actress!" she said enthusiastically.

"That's awesome," I said. "Well, let's practice having you take Joie in and out of her wheelchair, okay?"

She nodded. "Yes, I need to understand how this works."

Megan looked on with curiosity as I pointed to the strap that ran across the front of Joie's chest. "This gray strap has a red buckle on the side. What I need you to do is press it and it will open."

Nodding again, Megan did as I told her and it opened without a problem.

"Great. Now see those two metal circles on the side of the wheelchair?" I said, pointing to them.

"Yes."

"Well, those are called pins. They are what hold the aluminum bars in place on either side of Joie. This keeps her aligned in the center of those bars and steady in her wheels. Just pull those out, one at a time."

I held my hand open as she pulled the pins out and placed them in my hand. I put them in my pants pocket, which I often did so I didn't lose them.

"Okay, now all you have to do is lift the aluminum bar up and move it over the top of her to the other side."

Megan did just as I instructed, moving the bar from one side of Joie to the other.

"Now comes the fun part!" I said. "You get to lift Joie out of her wheelchair." I returned Megan's smile. "I'll show you first and then you can try."

I gently placed my hands near Joie's back. "You just place your hands under Joie's belly, like this, with one on either side to support her back end. Then you will gently lift her out and set her off to the side of the wheelchair."

Megan was watching intently, her eyebrows furrowed. "Oh yes, I see."

Once Joie was sitting off to the side, I said, "As you can see, part of her wheelchair looks sort of like a saddle with two openings. One leg fits into each opening. Now I'll show you how to place Joie back in her wheelchair."

Cupping my hand under Joie's belly once again, I lifted her back end and placed one leg then the other in each of the openings of the saddle. I moved the aluminum bar from the one side to the other. Reaching into my pocket, I pulled out the pins and put them back in place to secure the aluminum bar in place with the other one. Lastly, I put the gray strap around the front of Joie's chest, buckling it into place.

"See? Just like that and she is back in her wheelchair!"

"It seems easy enough to do," Megan said.

"Yes, it's really not that hard. Want to give it a try now by yourself?"

"I won't hurt her, will I?"

"No not at all. You just need to be gentle and go slow. But don't worry, I'll be right here to guide you."

Megan did it perfectly on the first try; more importantly, Joie didn't seem to mind. Still, we practiced a few more times.

"This is really neat how this works," she said, "and not hard to do."

I smiled. "Nope, not hard at all." It always touched my heart when I could share this experience with kids, teaching them about compassion by caring for a special needs pet. "We should probably give Joie a little break and let her rest."

"Yes, I think that's a good idea," Megan said, genuinely concerned for Joie's well-being.

We stayed seated on the floor, watching the flurry of action around us. Joie lay next to Megan as Megan stroked her back. They were forming a fast and sweet bond.

We watched as props were going back and forth from the dining room into the front hallway. Every now and then a crew member would walk into the kitchen and get one of the extras to help shoot a scene. Once a scene was ready I would hear the director shout, "Camera! Action!" to signal to everyone that it was time to be quiet.

They had just finished up a scene when a nice-looking man walked into the kitchen and over to me and Megan, his hand outstretched.

"Hi, you must be Barbara."

I got to my feet and shook his hand. "Yes, I am."

"I'm Gil Cates, the director of the film."

"It's great to meet you," I said, and realized I was a little nervous; after all, I had never met a director before. I hoped my hand wasn't too sweaty.

His smile put me at ease. "How long has Joie been in a wheelchair?"

"She's only been using it for about five months now. I adopted her last October. I did physical therapy with her first to help build up her strength before I introduced her to the wheelchair."

He patted the top of her head. "She's really cute. I think it's really great that you are helping her."

"Thank you, I enjoy taking care of these little ones." I gestured around the room, "And thank you for asking us to be a part of this."

Gil nodded. "The scene Joie will be taking part in is with a father—who's being played by Chris Mulkey—and his daughter, who as you know is being played by Megan. The father is about to leave for work and the daughter will be coming down the stairs from her bedroom to say goodbye to him."

I listened carefully, nodding my head up and down.

"What I'd like is for Joie to walk through the front hallway and meet Megan at the bottom of the stairway." Glancing at Joie, he said, "Is it hard to take the wheelchair off of her?"

"Not all that hard. Megan has been practicing."

"Can it be done within a matter of seconds, or can Megan easily pick up the wheelchair with Joie still in it?"

Looking at Megan I said, "Well, I think we can certainly practice that." Megan nodded in agreement. "Actually, it might work better to have Megan pick her up in her wheelchair instead of trying to take her out."

Megan chimed in. "I can practice lifting her up and holding her, Mr. Cates. I think that will work well."

Cates smiled. "Okay, let's go with it."

Turning his attention back to me, he said, "Thank you again for being here today and being a part of the movie. We will be shooting Joie's scene soon."

"You are very welcome."

As he walked back to the living room set, I immediately started showing Megan the proper way to pick Joie up and hold her while she was in her wheelchair.

I was somewhat apprehensive that she might not be able to hold Joie steady once she had her in her arms. The extra weight of the wheelchair and the fact that Joie could be a bit wiggly would likely feel awkward for Megan.

But she was very careful, taking her time, gently picking Joie up, holding her for a few moments, and then setting her back down again. She was doing a great job.

After she had practiced a bit I began to feel more at ease. I was about to sit down when a woman with funky purple glasses walked over and introduced herself as Jessica, a Video Graphic Coordinator for the film.

She was holding some stickers in her hands. "Is it okay if I dress Joie's wheelchair out in these racing stickers and this black and white duct tape?"

I wasn't sure why she wanted to do that, but I shrugged and told her it was fine. As she started to wrap the tape around the sides of the wheelchair, I said, "You know what? We actually live in Elkhart Lake and our little town is famous for its race track called 'Road America.'"

"Really? Well, then, this is very fitting!"

As Jessica continued dressing up the wheelchair, I glanced at the clock on the kitchen wall, unable to believe that we had been there for three hours already. The time was certainly flying by, but I didn't know how long Joie would last before she tuckered out. Thankfully, it was only a few moments later when a crew member came and got me, Joie and Megan and took us to the front entrance of the house.

We stood in the hallway as Cates explained how the scene would play out. Chris Mulkey would walk from the living room that was off to the side, and head for the front door. As he was doing this, Megan would come down the stairway while Joie would be walking in her wheelchair toward the bottom of the stairs. Once Megan got down to the last step, she would stop, pick Joie up, walk over to Chris, kiss him on the cheek, and tell him to have a good day.

It seemed like an easy enough scene to shoot and probably wouldn't take long either. I just hoped Joie would cooperate.

"Do you think you can entice Joie with a treat to get her to walk down the hallway? She won't be able to see you. You will need to be on the other side of the stairs in the dining room."

"I can certainly try that, but Joie isn't all that motivated by treats. I brought along a favorite toy of hers that has a squeaker in it—she will usually come to if I squeak it."

"Let's work with that then. Don't worry about the squeaking—we can edit that out later. You can also call out to her because we'll be able to edit that out too."

Hearing this was a relief. "Okay, sounds good."

I kissed the top of Joie's head and set her down on the floor near a crew member by the camera. He held the back of her wheelchair so she wouldn't follow as I took my place behind the stairway.

As we waited for the scene to begin, I could see Chris Mulkey standing across the hallway in the living room. Then I heard, "Quiet on the set! Camera! Action!"

What would ultimately be a fifteen-second scene took a little over an hour to shoot.

I thought Joie did pretty well for the most part, though I could tell toward the end of the hour that she was tired. Her gait was slower and she was lying down every chance she got.

"If you think she is up for it," Cates said, "I'd like to get one more shot of Joie coming from around the corner in the living room then down the hallway toward the front door."

"We can certainly try," I said, "I do think she is getting tired, though."

"I promise we will only try three times. If we don't get it, we will go without."

I nodded my consent.

The crew member held the back of Joie's wheelchair once again while I kneeled down on the tile floor in the center of the hallway and began calling her name.

The first two times Joie refused to walk; she simply sat down when Cates shouted, "Action!" Luckily for us, she decided she would give it one last hurrah. She rolled around the corner with enthusiasm and almost rolled right into my lap! I hugged her and whispered in her ear, "Good job, sweetheart. You did it."

Cates said, "She did a great job! Thank you again. I really appreciate your taking the time to be here today."

"Absolutely!" I said as I scooped Joie up, "It was really fun. Thanks again for asking us to be a part of this."

As I walked off the set, I saw Jeff standing in the dining room doorway.

"Great job, Barbara and Joie! Thanks again."

"You bet! It was a wonderful experience and one I'll remember for a long time to come. Would it be okay if I took a picture of you and Joie together? I'd love to write about this experience on my blog."

He was so gracious. "Yes, of course, I'd be happy to do that."

I placed Joie, still in her wheelchair, into his arms, then quickly grabbed my camera and snapped two pictures.

As he handed Joie back to me he said, "I'll be in touch."

Before leaving, I asked Megan if I could have her mailing address. "I want to send you a copy of each of my children's books that I wrote about my first dog, Frankie, who was in a wheelchair."

"Oh, thank you so much! I'd really like that," she said. "I didn't know you were writer. That is so neat!"

She got a piece of paper and a pen from her mom and jotted down her address. We said goodbye and I wished her luck with the rest of the movie.

As I held Joie in my arms, walking past the front of the house again, on my left I saw two trailers. I assumed they were for the actors. Sean Astin, who was playing the other main character in the film, didn't appear to be on set that day. But when I walked past the second trailer, the door was open. I saw Mimi Rogers, who also stars in the film as the wife of Chris Mulkey. She was sitting on a sofa reading.

I couldn't stop smiling as I walked down the street and back to my car. I really was in awe of this once in a lifetime experience. It was surreal in so many ways.

It had also been a big day for Joie. She stayed awake while I strapped her into her car seat, but within minutes of my pulling away from the curb her eyes were dropping. As I drove home,

I replayed the entire morning and suddenly found myself overcome with emotions, not the least of which was pride for Joie. Could this be, I wondered, the reason she had found her way to me?

The way I saw it, Joie would be representing all special needs pets; her scene in the movie, which depicted a dog who despite being in wheelchair had a family who loved and cared for her, would hopefully educate others that these dogs can live quality lives if given a chance. It was as if through the film Joie had continued the mission that Frankie and I had started.

CHAPTER SIXTEEN

Devastating News

I floated for days on the good feelings of having taken part in the movie, *The Surface*. But in between those moments of joy, my mind was in high gear, trying to figure out what was next. I couldn't seem to just rest in what *was* without searching for what may be ahead.

I scanned the shelves of books in my writing cottage, hoping one would jump out at me. I had read most of them before, but I'd found that the right information comes to us when we're ready for it. Maybe there was something here that would help me learn to just "be" during this transitional period.

Sure enough, my eyes landed on Sue Bender's, *Stretching Lessons*, which I'd read years ago. Now I slid it off the shelf and opened it to a page where I'd left a sticky tab. I was struck by a particular sentence, which I read aloud: "It's easier to know what I don't want. It's much harder to know what I want."

Well, that certainly struck a chord! Bender went on to relay advice she had received from a friend: "Practice feeling good where you are." Wow. There was so much truth is this, I thought. How often we spend so much time in the future and not the present and thus miss out on the joy of being in the moment. How often we don't have patience to just *allow* our lives to unfold as they are meant to. I starred at the page, trying to let these wise words of wisdom seep deeply into my consciousness.

The more I thought about Bender's book, the more I felt my body relax into its wisdom. It was something I continually practiced, though I lost my way now and then—usually when I came up against others' standards out in the world. Standards put upon us by society of how we *should* live our lives, instead of following what *feels* right for us individually.

This time, I was determined to take Bender's advice to heart. I wanted to feel better and accept where I was right now, instead of thinking I had to figure everything out right away. I silently set my intention to work with the flow of being instead of against it. But little did I know that my life was about to turn upside down again.

It was just a week after being on the set of the movie that I found myself nervously awaiting news of what might be wrong with Joie. The morning before nothing seemed out of the ordinary. As I prepared her food she sat near my feet and looked up at me, like most dogs waiting for a meal. But when I set her bowl down for her to eat, she kept looking at me, not paying attention to the fact her food was right in front of her.

This was unusual because she usually gobbled her food down rather quickly.

"What's wrong, little one?" I said as I took note that she was holding her head cocked to the side in a peculiar way. Could she not bend her head down, I wondered? Picking up her bowl, I held it near her mouth, but she turned away.

Something was wrong. I knew enough about IVDD that this could be a sign of a rupture or tear in her neck area. I silently prayed this wasn't the case.

I was able to get her in to see our local veterinarian that morning. Joie didn't indicate any signs of pain when Dr. B examined her. But because of her history of IVDD he referred us to Dr. R, a neurologist about an hour away.

Our appointment was the following morning. After Dr. R examined her he suggested a CT scan. He said Joie would need to be sedated for the procedure and had to stay overnight.

I drove back home and after a restless night with not much sleep, I was now waiting for Dr. R to call with the results. I can still see myself, sitting on the edge of my bed, looking out into our backyard as Dr. R gave me the news I didn't want to hear. Joie had a moderate tear in her neck.

"There are also two other areas of concern from the scan. But I want to consult with a few colleagues of mine first. I want to get their opinions before discussing those findings with you," he said.

"Oh no, what is it?"

"I'm not quite sure and that's why I want to first talk with some fellow colleagues. I won't be able to talk with them until this evening, but will call you again first thing in the morning."

I didn't like the fact I had to wait again but said, "Okay."

Hanging up the phone I felt lost in a swirl of emotions. How could all of this have happened so fast? I wondered. How could it be that just the week before I was so happy and now felt in fear that something seriously could be wrong with Joie? I tried to tell myself to not jump to conclusions, silently praying that everything was going to turn out fine.

Around ten the next morning my cell phone finally rang.

"Good morning, Barb," Dr. R said, "I had a chance to talk with two other neurologists last night. There are many complications and I think it would be best if I can show you the scan and go over the details with you in person."

I started to cry, but after a few deep breaths I managed to say, "Okay, yes, I can do that. I'm going to call my mom first and see if she can come with me."

The word "complications" scared me, and I wanted someone with me, both for comfort and to make sure I caught and understood everything the doctor said.

"I understand," he said. "When you get here, just let the receptionist know. Whenever that is, I will make time for you."

Two hours later, my mom and I were sitting in a dark exam room. My heart breaking, I looked on at Dr. R's computer screen that showed the inside of Joie's little body.

"This is a very unusual case," Dr. R said. "I've never seen anything like this."

My heart began beating fast in my chest and my head spun as if I was in a bad dream. Pointing to the screen, he showed me the first area of concern—the lower portion of her spine near her tail. He told me her spine was dying.

But he was even more worried about the second area. His finger moved until it was pointed toward Joie's head, specifically to a greyish mass in her head. It appeared to be a bubble on the stem of her brain.

"Without surgery, I can't say for sure what it is. It could be nothing, but in my opinion, and having conferred with two other neurologists, I feel it likely is a tumor."

All I could do was stare at the screen and shake my head from side-to-side. I couldn't believe what he was telling me.

"The most immediate and pressing concern is the tear in her neck," he said. "I can do surgery to repair the rupture, but I have to caution you that because of the situation with the bubble on the stem of her brain, this is very risky. Doing the surgery may cause the bubble to burst." He paused for a moment, then said, "And she would likely die on the table if that happens."

By now it felt like I had left my body. I couldn't think straight and was trying to wrap my brain around everything that Dr. R had just said. It was all so surreal. I couldn't take my eyes off the scanned image of Joie on the screen; perhaps if I starred at it long enough it would all go away and I'd wake up.

Dr. R got up to turn the lights on and as he did, I felt this sudden urge to bolt from the room. I wanted to find Joie, who was still in the back of the clinic somewhere, grab her and run as far away as I could. I wanted to pretend like this wasn't really happening.

But I knew it was, and I had to deal with it the best I could.

I put my hands on the end of the exam table and laid my head down. "This sucks," I said. I felt my mom's hand rub my back, trying to soothe me.

"I know," Dr. R said. "I'll give you time to think this over. I'm supposed to go out of town tomorrow, but if you decide to do the surgery, I will cancel everything. I have to be honest though and tell you that I think things for Joie could progress quite fast. Addressing the rupture now may work and provide her some time. But you are likely looking at another surgery sooner rather than later to address the bubble on the stem of her brain. And again, it is a risky surgery. I just want you to understand what is at stake here."

By this point I was too numb to do anything but nod my head up and down. Dr. R stepped out of the room, and I just sat there, staring straight ahead, trying to make sense of it all. My head knew what the right answer was, but I knew it was going to take some work to convince my heart.

Time felt like it was crawling by while at the same time it felt like it was spinning out of control. Finally I said, "I just don't know what to do, Mom."

My mom didn't answer right away. "Do you want to know what I'd do if it were my dog?"

Turning to look at her, I said almost in a whisper, "Yes. What would you do?"

"I'd take her home." It was a simple statement filled with compassion and love for her daughter who was in so much pain. She always seemed to know exactly what my heart was feeling. She was right. This was what I wanted to do.

I opted to try conservative treatment, something I'd learned about years earlier when Frankie was diagnosed with IVDD. It would mean keeping Joie crated 24/7 and only letting her out for bathroom breaks. Keeping a dog with a ruptured disc as confined and quiet as possible was often helpful when surgery wasn't an option.

After talking to Dr. R, he supported my decision. He also sent me home with a list of medications to help Joie with the pain. As my mom, Joie and I left the clinic, I had every hope in the world that this would all work out. I knew I would certainly give it my all to help her recover.

I dropped my mom off in the parking lot of Fleet Farm, where she had met me that morning. Once I got home, I carefully got Joie out of the car, carried her into the house and laid her gently in her kennel. She was already on a few medications from having stayed at the clinic, so I had time to call a pharmacy and fill the other prescriptions.

Joie was only a few feet away from me as I sat at the kitchen table and Googled "pharmacies that fill compound medications." Suddenly I sensed something wasn't right and looked over at Joie. I noticed her belly going in and out quite fast, and her breathing was labored.

With a sinking feeling in my stomach, I immediately called Dr. R's clinic and told him about Joie's breathing. He instructed me to take her pulse and though I don't recall what it was I do remember Dr. R stating that it was quite high.

"Can you try taking Joie out of her kennel and see if she will stand?" Although I didn't know it at the time, this was something she had still been able to do while at the clinic.

"Okay. I'll need to set my phone down."

"That's okay. Take your time. I can wait."

When I reached into Joie's kennel to pick her up she yelped out in pain. I couldn't bear to hear her like this. I opted instead to try and see if she would stand in her kennel. I placed my hands under her and gently tried to help her up on all fours, but she was just too weak and her legs buckled under her. As I guided her to her side again so she could rest, she plopped over like a rag doll and let out another yelp.

I grabbed my phone again. "Did you hear that? She can't stand and appears to be very weak."

"Yes," he said. "I'm afraid things are progressing more quickly than I thought."

By now tears were flowing down my face. "But this fast?" I didn't understand and truly thought Joie would get better with lots of rest and care from me. "I don't know what to do."

"You can bring her back in and I can do the surgery right away if you'd like." He paused. "Or I'm afraid to say the other option is to euthanize her."

In my heart I knew the answer. "She has so many other complications, it just does not seem fair to put her through all this..."

"I understand," he said.

I starred at the floor before looking at Joie again in her kennel. Though my heart was breaking, I knew what the right thing was to do. I couldn't let her suffer.

"I just can't do this to her," I said, then hesitated a moment longer before I finally said, "I think I need to let her go."

With kindness and compassion in his voice he said, "I think you are making the right decision, Barb. Would you like me to call ahead to your vet and let them know you are bringing Joie in?"

"Yes, I would really appreciate that. Thank you."

"I'm so sorry, Barb. I truly am."

"I know. I know. I am too."

As soon as I hung up on the phone I burst out crying, but it was short-lived. Trying to get it together, I grabbed a tissue and blew my nose, then walked over to Joie's kennel. Resting my hand on her soft body, I leaned over and kissed the side of her tiny face.

"I'm so sorry, Joie. I'm so sorry."

I grabbed her pink blanket and as gently as I could, I lifted her out of the kennel, tucking the blanket under her belly and wrapping it around her.

I had called John earlier, as soon as I realized something was wrong with Joie; now, I called to let him know that I was on the way to the vet's office to let her go. He was upset by the news, but not all that surprised.

"I'll meet you there as soon as I can. I'm just finishing up with an appointment. Drive safe, honey."

"I will."

The bottom half of the portable kennel I'd used to transport her to and from Dr. R's clinic was still in the backseat of the car. I had rolled up bath towels on either side to be sure I had kept her immobile as possible. Now, I placed it in the front passenger seat then gently laid her back in the kennel.

As I drove down our street, I was still crying. But then I remembered the day I had to say goodbye to Frankie. I didn't want Joie to worry about me, so I pulled myself together, telling myself I could cry all I wanted later. Right now I had to be strong for her.

For the next six miles to the vet clinic, I stroked Joie's body with my free hand and told her over and over again how much I loved her.

When I arrived at the clinic, John was already waiting inside. An hour later, we were walking out of the exam room of the vet's office, leaving behind our beautiful Joie to be privately cremated.

My heart was heavy with grief. It would take some time to really understand why she was only in my life for such a short time, and after I had worked so hard to get her strong. At that moment, the reason didn't matter; Joie was gone and she had taken any sense of direction I had gained along with her.

CHAPTER SEVENTEEN

The Decision

The next three days were a blur. I was numb, but in a way I didn't mind because I really didn't want to feel anything anyway. I wished it were all a bad dream.

The one thing I did know is that I had to be gentle with myself, allowing myself to move through my grief at my own pace. Grief. That word sure was showing up in my life a lot lately.

The odd thing was that I didn't want to talk about Joie. After Frankie died it was all I had wanted to do. I felt compelled to let her fans know, and within hours of her passing, I had posted a tribute on my blog and Facebook. Though it was difficult to write, it was also deeply therapeutic.

But with Joie, the words wouldn't come. Not for lack of loving her, but more that her death was unexpected. I didn't quite know how to express what I was feeling, nor did I really want to try. All I felt was this deep, empty hollow pit in my heart, and somehow, wallowing in my sadness made me feel connected to her.

If I wrote about her, I'd have to acknowledge she was gone. I wasn't ready for that yet.

Every bit of joy I'd experienced over the past six years now felt ripped out of me, and I feared it might never return.

All those years I'd worked tirelessly, but with much enthusiasm and compassion as I spread a positive message with Frankie at my side. She was a big reason I had bloomed into who I am today. In some ways, I had hoped Joie would pick up where Frankie left off so I could walk the same path—one that had fulfilled me in a way I'd never experienced before.

How could I have had my purpose all figured out, only to now feel like I had no clue to what I wanted next? The question plagued me, and at times, drove me crazy as it spun in a loop in my mind. Joie's passing seemed to have magnified a whisper that had been trying to get my attention for some time. I knew well enough from my earlier self-exploration that if I didn't tune in to what my inner voice was trying to tell me it would only continue to get louder.

Joie's death reminded me not only of Frankie, but how much of my identity was wrapped up in being part of a team. While I felt a sense of relief after retiring Frankie so I could slow down, I just wasn't sure how to move forward in a new direction. On the other hand, I also wasn't ready to dig deep and figure out why it scared me so to be on my own. Addressing the unknown was too uncomfortable.

And then there were days when I felt cheated out of many more years with Joie. I'd find myself having a pity party, with so many emotions, most of them unpleasant, swirling around in me. I even worried I'd never want to write again, which might have been most frightening of all.

Many days I vacillated back and forth, often ignoring all the thoughts that seemed to be running across my mind at a rapid speed. It was becoming increasingly obvious that these feelings weren't going to go away on their own. I had to face them.

It was going to take honest work on my part. I also knew how impatient I can be, wanting to know *now* that everything I was going through was for a very good reason. I wanted to be assured that this was all for a divine purpose.

Somehow, someway, I had to get back to that confident and serene place within myself—this place of trusting that this was all part of a master plan for my life. I knew this meant allowing myself to feel vulnerable and trust in the process. If I could only bring myself to look within, I'd regain my sense of self.

About a week later, an answer came loud and clear. I knew I couldn't ignore it. It felt urgent. Something was telling me it was time to take a serious break.

This scared me even though I could feel in my heart it was the right thing to do. But I had worked so hard building a wonderful community of like-minded people through my writing, blog, social media avenues and school visits. How could I walk away from it, even if only for a short time?

A part of me felt a deep sense of obligation to others who had trusted in my work and followed me. They had supported me in one way or another all these years. I felt like I'd be letting them down.

Still, I felt strongly that I needed to step away; I just wasn't exactly sure how to go about it. For help, I turned to Dan.

I'd gotten to know Dan over the past two years, having taken many of his online courses. In the process I had learned that many writers feel this incredible, constant pressure to always be connecting in some way with their audience, whether online or off. While the Internet has served as an amazing way for writers to put their voice out into the world, it often ends up becoming an all-consuming quest to be seen in a world where there is so much noise. Still, it was extremely difficult to walk away, even for a short while. Being able to interact with these writers and hear Dan's advice to them had helped me accept my own transition period. I had also come to think of him as a mentor. I admired his honesty and how much he cared about helping others. He is truly someone who walks his talk and lives his life in a meaningful way.

Before my courage up and left, I began composing an email to Dan, explaining why I was strongly considering stepping back from my writing for a while. I also shared with him that Joie had passed away recently and I needed space to grieve and sort things out. When I was at a loss for words, I'd stare out the window of the writing cottage and try to rein in my conflicting feelings.

When I finished, my index finger hovered over the enter key of the keyboard. I knew once I sent the message there would be no turning back. While I was worried what Dan might say, a voice inside me quietly cheered me on.

Taking a deep breath, I finally hit send. My heart pounded in my chest for a few moments. It was a huge step. I really didn't know how soon I'd hear back from Dan or what his advice would be.

Just a few moments later, I heard my computer ping with a new email. Glancing at the screen, I was surprised to see it was from Dan: *I'm available for a few minutes this morning if you'd like to talk. Feel free to give me a call.*

With a sigh of relief, I immediately grabbed my cell phone and punched in Dan's number. It only rang once before I heard his voice.

After thanking him for taking the time to speak to me, I reiterated everything that had been going on—Joie's death, the emptiness I was feeling and my need to step back from my writing and social media.

"I'm scared of losing everything I've worked so hard to build," I said, "Can I really just *stop?*"

A part of me really expected Dan to try to talk me out it, so I was surprised when he said, "I think you should take the time you need. Do you have an idea of how long that will be?" I didn't hesitate, as I had already thought about this. "Actually, yes, I'm thinking at least a month, perhaps two, because my husband and I have a vacation planned for mid-October. I want to take it one day at a time and see how I feel once we return."

Dan was supportive, encouraging me to follow my heart. He also said I should simply let my readers know what to expect by writing a simple blog post.

The advice was so simple, yet profound, and I felt myself relaxing into my chair. There was no denying this was the right thing to do. I genuinely cared about my readers and didn't want to let them down. But I also felt strongly that if I tried to keep writing, I wouldn't be serving them in a positive way.

It was time for me to refill my well. What appeared as a huge mountain in front of me before I talked to Dan was now a welcome, beautiful hill—a hill I could climb at my leisure and rest often along the way. A place I could sink into silence and open my mind to possibilities. A place I could enjoy the view without having to share it.

Though I still worried about what might happen if I did not stay connected on a daily basis, it was a risk I knew I had to take. I wanted more than anything to find my way back to my sense of self.

I was ready to take the plunge into stillness.

Part Two

The Pause

CHAPTER EIGHTEEN

Walking Away

Dan's assurance that I should follow my heart and take a hiatus from my writing was a gift.

An hour after our conversation—and mulling many thoughts around in my mind—I sat down to write a blog post to my loyal and faithful readers.

Dear Friends,

I've been giving thought these past few days about something I realize now that I should have likely done a year ago. But I kept pushing down the wee voice inside me that was trying to get my attention—the one that said it was time to slow down and re-evaluate where I want to go next in my life.

Joie's unexpected passing has been my wake-up call.

I'm taking a sabbatical. This will be a private journey back to the center of my heart. It's time for me to once again be still, listen and explore. I believe this is Joie's gift to me. It's also how Joyful Paws came to be when in 2005 I paused for three months, guided by a life coach, and taking time to explore what it was that would bring me more joy and fulfillment.

Cassie Jo, my chocolate Lab I had at that time, gave me the gift of understanding that taking time to search my soul for answers was exactly what I needed to do. It's time for me to once again honor the gift of pausing.

I won't be posting to my blog and I will be taking a break from Facebook and other social media outlets. I'm also putting my newsletter on hold. I plan to be away at least through September, and likely October. But I will check back in at the end of September to let you know where I'm at.

I plan to continue to write, but will write just for me in my private journal. It's my hope that this will help me uncover the next leg in my journey. I have some ideas of what I want to explore. I also feel a strong sense that I want to close the chapter in my life and my work around Frankie and Joie. Not completely, but I need to re-evaluate how I will move forward in a new way with this.

This is, of course, where I am at this very moment. I'm making a conscious effort to not put any expectations on what is going to come from this time of self-exploration. Instead, I want to really listen deeply for clues that are likely within.

And dear friends, I do believe I know one thing for sure—that I will love another special needs dachshund again. I feel quite certain of that. But for now, I will honor Joie's gift of taking this time just for me.

Lastly, I want to say my deepest heartfelt thank you to all of you and your outpouring of love for the passing of Joie—so many of you shared beautiful sentiments on my blog, on Facebook and in emails to me.

I know you understand the profound loss of our special animal friends, as you've each been through this at least once in your lives, too. It's something we can't ever escape. As much as it hurts to lose them, I want to love another again when the time is right. I look forward to experiencing that joy again someday soon.

You are all a gift to me. I want you to know this. Again, I'll check back in at the end of September.

Until then, be well, choose joy, and follow your heart.

With love and gratitude,
Barbara

The moment I hit publish a huge weight lifted from my shoulders. It was, in a small but significant way, the first step to healing my broken and confused heart.

The next two months were now mine to just *be*. It felt wonderful, though I still had some apprehension about all this time looming in front of me. I'd become so used to having several lists going to keep up with my work schedule and day-to-day activities; now I wondered how I was going to fill my days. Sometimes, "to just *be*" felt more overwhelming than being overwhelmed with things to do.

That evening, John, Nikki, and I sat around the dinner table, chatting about our day. Suddenly Nikki blurted out, "I've made a decision to move into my own apartment."

While I expected this at some point, I was surprised that it was happening just three short months after she'd come to live with us. Though a part of me had been craving more quiet time, Nikki's news hit me hard. I had just lost Joie, and now I was losing her too.

I moved the food around on my plate, not looking up, trying to hold in the tears that sat so close to the surface. She happily chatted on about the apartment she'd found and the date she planned on moving. It was all happening so fast.

My emotions overcame me and I couldn't hold back the tears any longer. I jumped back from the kitchen table, running out onto the deck, and plunked myself down in an Adirondack chair.

I wanted to try and sort out what I was feeling, but I didn't have the opportunity, as John and Nikki were right behind me. The tears were flowing fast, despite my best effort to control them.

Like Joie's death, Nikki's departure had come without any warning, and in that moment it was almost too much to bear.

"I'm so sorry. I didn't mean to hurt you," Nikki said, trying to comfort me as she sat on the arm of the chair and put her arm around my shoulders.

What made it even more difficult was that John, Nikki and I had had somewhat of a blowout the Friday before. Nikki had promised to have dinner with us that evening and hang out around the chiminea afterward. I recall it being a celebration for something, although the reason escapes me now. When she didn't show up and didn't call, we were hurt. Now I wondered if perhaps that was her reason for wanting to move out.

"Is it something we said or haven't done?" I asked.

"No, not at all. I just think it's time for me to do this. I've been giving it thought for a few weeks now. On one hand, I'm scared to move out, but in another way, I want to prove to myself that I can make it on my own."

While I was upset, and feeling it more keenly because of the recent loss of Joie, I did understand what she was saying. After all, I was feeling similar emotions as I tried to figure out what I wanted for my own life.

The more we talked, the more I knew she was making the right decision—not only for herself, but for John and me also. We had worked hard to respect each other's boundaries, and although we had some trying times, we had all grown in ways we never imagined and in many ways had become our own family unit. Still, we knew the longer she stayed, the greater the risk that we wouldn't be able to preserve our relationship. The more I thought about it, the more I realized it would be nice for me and John to have our house to ourselves again.

The next morning, the official first day of my sabbatical, I woke to find a gift on the kitchen table. On the card next to it, I recognized the handwriting as Nikki's. Beneath the envelope was a mint green, cream, and cocoa checkered journal with the image of a tea cup on the cover.

Knowing I'd be writing for myself for a while, Nikki's gift couldn't have been more perfect. Journaling had served me well in the past as a way of expressing myself and helping me work through my feelings.

Deeply touched, I opened the envelope and pulled out the card. *The best things in life are free. Shine on.* It was signed with love from Nikki and John.

Smiling, I picked up the journal and ran my hand across the cover. It felt like I'd just been handed a million bucks. Holding the journal to my chest, I closed my eyes and felt loved and understood.

Eager to begin filling the pages, I could barely wait for the water to boil for my morning cup of tea. As soon as it was ready, I grabbed my new journal, headed to the living room and sat down in the far corner of the sofa.

Before I started to let my thoughts flow, I looked into the kitchen to see that Kylie was lying on the olive green rug, gazing out the front door. It was her favorite spot to sit most days. I smiled. She was so often my rock with her quiet, calm presence— just being near her always brings me back to my center, if only for a moment.

Turning my attention to my tea I realized I'd not yet read the quote that was included at the end of the string of each Yogi teabag. They always seemed to provide just the right wisdom I needed. It read, "Live and let live." That is right on, I thought. My "job" these next two months was to do just that—allow myself to just be and tune into my heart.

As I took my pen in hand a plethora of emotions were running amuck in my mind, all vying for my attention. I was scared, excited, feeling somewhat odd, happy, sad, and hopeful—just to name a few! It was certainly a crazy, unsettled place to be inside my head.

Staring at the blank white, lined page, it was as if there was this mystery before me, and I was a character in it. I had lost all clarity and was looking for any and all clues back to a path of fulfillment.

To my advantage, I knew well enough, having gone through this years ago with a life coach guiding me, that this all takes time. I just had to remember that open space and solitude were my friends.

As I sank into the present moment, my journal resting on the arm of the sofa, many of my scrambled thoughts started to find their way onto the page. I tried not to censor them and just let them have a voice. Every now and then, I'd look out the patio door into the backyard. The locust tree, still full with leaves, was swaying in the wind.

When I tuned into my heart, I still had that hollow feeling, yet I could feel that a shift was taking place, too. Just like the wind when it changes direction, I was ready (for the most part) to begin exploring what was next for me.

For as long as I can remember, I've felt a deep connection with animals. Open to what more I could learn from them, I had in the past considered exploring animal communication.

But whenever I thought about it, doubt set in. I didn't doubt for one moment that communicating with animals is possible—I'd had experienced signs from both Cassie Jo and Frankie—but did I really have that ability? And if I did, what would other people think?

I didn't have the answers to those questions, I decided to not force it, and let it simmer. It was something I decided I could look further into should the idea keep surfacing.

My thoughts turned to the way being around animals had always brought me comfort and peace; they grounded me like nothing else. It made me think about a place called Villa Loretto, which I'd always wanted to visit but never found the time.

Villa Loretto is a nursing home about a half hour from where I live; but what makes it most interesting is that it has on the property a small zoo. It is run by nuns and they have many different animals—chickens, donkeys, rabbits, horses, goats, llamas, geese, birds and pigs—all of whom serve as a type of therapy for the residents. It's also open to the public to come and enjoy at no cost, though donations are encouraged to help with feeding and caring for the animals.

Now that I had my days free, I decided I would make it a point to visit in the next few weeks. As I scribbled the plan in my journal, a sense of anticipation welled up within me. I felt like I had when I was a young school girl, excited about an impending field trip. It was going to be fun to bust out of my normal day-to-day routine and make plans for this special outing.

While it was a healthy release to examine my emotions and struggles on the pages of my journal, it was also tiring. I closed the cover without judgment, knowing that letting go of negative energy was an often exhausting but necessary part of the process. It had to be done if I wanted to allow new energy and possibilities to come into my life.

One of the hardest things I had to work through was my grief, and as much as I didn't want to, I knew I had to deal with the numerous unanswered emails in my inbox. Most of them were compassionate notes of condolences about Joie.

While I was grateful for those who had come to love Joie, it felt like a daunting task to reply to everyone. It would also force me to deal with the pain I was still in and the many unanswered questions of my own life. For a moment I thought that perhaps I didn't need to write back, but I felt obligated.

Instead of going to the computer, I opened my journal again and without much conscious thought found myself writing: *My little Joie, my little Butterduck* (a name I accidentally called her one day when I combined two nicknames—Buttercup and Little Duck), *I'm so sorry I couldn't have done more for you.*

There it was—staring back at me—the intense reason for my pain. It was like a ton of bricks sitting on my chest. The guilt I felt that I somehow failed Joie. I sat in these very uncomfortable, overwhelming feelings, praying to Spirit to please help me let go of something I probably couldn't have changed.

In the next moment, I thought about a book I had begun reading the night before. It was called *Animal Voices,* by animal communicator Dawn Baumann Brunke, and it was still sitting right where I had left it, on the ottoman in front of the sofa. I picked it up and re-read two passages that had struck a chord with me. I had even dog-eared the pages so I could easily find them again, and I was being called to do so now.

When we are open to communication with animals, we are open to deeper layers of ourselves.

When we learn how to use all our senses to listen to animals, we will find out how to listen, to be our authentic self as well.

Cassie Jo and then Frankie had certainly guided me to paying more attention to what mattered most to me. Each, in her own way, had also given me the courage to start living with more intent and integrity. As a result, I was now much more comfortable in my own skin.

While I was still grappling with why Joie had to leave so soon, I began to sense that perhaps an answer really was buried deep down inside me. It was a reminder of how important it was for me to take time to do what I could to uncover it.

CHAPTER NINETEEN

Learning to Slow Down

One would think that taking two months off would feel like heaven. But what I didn't anticipate was that my emotions would feel as if they were riding a roller coaster.

Most people, myself included, have become so accustomed to being on the go all the time that it is very difficult to slow down. It felt counterintuitive and as if I was being unproductive. And there was this guilt that kept trying to convince me that I really should be *doing* something.

I had to work hard to trust that this was part of the process. I needed to be open to the restlessness because in all likelihood this was part of what I needed to understand and learn. After all, how can clarity find us if we fill our minds day in and day out with busyness? I knew that in order to move toward a place of deeper awareness and the answers I was seeking, I needed to make friends with stillness. How that was exactly going to look, I had no idea.

Suddenly, I felt the need to examine my every thought and deed. Since deciding to take a day to visit Villa Loretto, I had begun to think about other places in the area I could explore. While this felt in one sense like a "to-do," I realized that it was also a way in which I could give myself permission to enjoy, relax and let my mind wander to new places of discovery.

I made a promise to myself I would continue to journal everyday as part of my inner soul work. I also dug out the dry erase board that had been tucked away in a corner of the writing cottage and began making a list of places I wanted to see or things I wanted to do that would serve as another way for me to pause, listen and trust the unfolding of the process. It was my hope that each part would act as stepping stones, organically leading me to what was next. Though making a list initially felt like what I did to keep myself on track in my working world, I realized the list would help me look forward while at the same time help me stay grounded in the present.

My list contained the following:

1. Visit animals at Villa Loretto.
2. Explore animal communication.
3. Schedule a massage.
4. Visit friend and life coach, Diane.
5. Explore workshop ideas to offer in the future to women (note: initially this felt like a goal, but I allowed myself to just jot it down without feeling pressure to follow through on it).
6. Plant honeysuckle to attract hummingbirds.
7. Drive the Kettle Moraine scenic route and find a spot to stop and journal.
8. Explore the topic of past life regression and listen to CD.
9. Order *The Animal Wisdom Tarot Cards* by Dawn Baumann Brunke.
10. Listen to *Spirit Guides* CDs by Sonia Choquette.
11. Pick a day to journal along the shores of Lake Michigan.

I had made a similar list a few years earlier under the guidance of a life coach, and I felt it was an excellent way to help me uncover what my soul was trying to tell me.

I honestly never thought I'd find myself in this place of unknowns once again. In many ways I thought I'd had it all figured out. But I would slowly come to realize that being in transition is what the ebb and flow of life is all about—and what leads us down the path of deeper discovery about ourselves.

With my list now complete, I propped it up against a small table. I had written each item in a different color, which made it feel alive and happy. I smiled, excited about all the possibilities before me and curious about what avenues this might open.

So I was a bit surprised when the next morning I awoke in a funk. Guilt was eating at me again. It was as if there were two people inside my head fighting back and forth, one worrying what others would say (i.e. "Must be nice to take a long break," or "I couldn't possibly do that because I have to work," or "I have kids so this is impossible."), the other (who I would learn is the wiser part of myself) saying "Hey, this is my life! This is what is right for *me* and what I feel I need to do. Everyone's life is different. What works for one person, may not work for another. But we each have to figure that out in our own way."

I knew this battle in my head was all a game. It would be easy to come up with all types of excuses instead of digging in and doing the hard work I needed to do.

Again, because I'd been through this before, I was pretty sure I'd grow and evolve from this experience. And I was pretty sure it would lead to me being an even better version of myself.

I thought more and more about how so often we say we are "busy." It's as if some of us wear this as a badge of honor. Busy seems to have morphed into something that is *expected* of us. If we aren't busy with multi-tasking and onto the next thing before we even finish the last, we are viewed as being lazy.

So many thoughts were flying through my mind again as I sat with my journal, this being only the second day of my sabbatical. I thought about how many people had reached out to me via Faceook and email. Many telling me they understood I was grieving the loss of Joie and they knew it was the reason I needed to step away for a while.

While yes, that was true, it was so much deeper. Joie's death was a call to awaken on another level. It was time to start paying attention and really listen to what I'd been ignoring for too long out of fear. Those whispers inside my mind had played like a recorder over and over, and time again I pushed them away…until the death of my sweet girl Joie made me realize I could no longer do that.

How often we discount the inner messages vying for our attention. Instead we become comfortable in feeling uncomfortable. To explore a new way of becoming looms before us like a steep hill that we feel we simply don't have the energy to climb. At least this has been the case for me more than once in my life.

While I was willing to finally begin the climb again, I knew it would take much concerted effort and all the energy I had. Trying to explain this to others would have meant expending some of that precious energy, and this, I was unwilling to do. I didn't think I could find the words to convey the many emotions I was feeling. And the truth was, I didn't feel I *had* to explain myself right now.

It was important for me to honor this time to be alone with my thoughts and figure out as much as I could on my own without outside interference.

While I was ready in many ways to pay attention to the small voice inside of me, beckoning me to let go of the last chapter of my life, I was scared to sound it out loud. It would make it real and I wasn't sure I was ready for that. So my journal, for the time being, was my safe place to open to all my fears.

As I did so, I kept reminding myself that only by addressing my emotions would I be able to let them go. One of my greatest challenges, I realized, was reconciling myself to the fact I had not found the *purpose of my life*, but a purpose for a period of my life.

When I watched in curious observation, it was like there was a board of committee members sitting at a long table inside my head. And oh, did they have discussions! Their topic? Me, and what they felt was best for my life. They all had a different opinion! Trying to respect each of them, I'd scribble like mad onto the blank page of my journal. I also tried hard to not judge what was coming out of my pen, but instead look at it as a way of releasing the mixed messages. I hoped this would all eventually make some sort of sense.

Something else that didn't make sense was that while I was craving time alone, I was also struggling with feeling lonely. But was it true loneliness, or was I just afraid to be alone and listen to what my soul was trying to share with me? This was a clue to keep allowing myself to move through each and every feeling, even though it felt awkward.

I wrote like a mad woman in my journal, trying to capture every thought that was firing rapidly through my mind. "The clock is ticking—the day is flying by. There is so much stuff in my head. I need to get it out. No filters! Just write!"

When I reread what I'd just written it felt like I was scolding myself on the page. But I wanted more than anything to move through the built-up gunk and get to a more stable place within myself. I also knew this was going to take time. I couldn't rush it, but learn to just be with it.

The next day I decided to practice more of being and listening, which was the major point of my sabbatical after all.

This led my mind to thinking about adopting another dachshund with IVDD. Even though I knew I had to wait because of another promise to John, I couldn't help myself thinking about caring for, and loving, another dog.

We were planning on a vacation, this time to Asheville, North Carolina, and I said I wouldn't bring another dog into our life until we returned. Our trip was more than a month away, and I didn't know how I was going to wait that long. My love of dachshunds, especially those with special needs, felt like such an integral part of me.

I wrote out all of my hopes and fears in that journal, and was often surprised by what came out. My next dachshund, I wrote, was one I wanted all to myself. I didn't want to share her with others like I had done with Frankie. I didn't want to take her to schools or libraries. I wanted her to be *my* companion. This was exactly what I had been wrestling with when I had Joie, but was too afraid to examine closer.

While I still loved the idea of another therapy dog, I felt this time it would be best to pay attention to what the dog wanted, even if it was a completely different life. If she was meant to be a therapy dog, well then that is what we would do, but if not, I knew I had to work on being okay with that, too.

There it was, in black and white on the page. I was listening to what my heart was telling me. I owned the truth of what I felt was next for me. It was a good start. But one thought I couldn't seem to shake was worrying that my change of direction might disappoint others. Their imaginary voices echoed in my head, and they seemed to expect I'd continue the work I had been doing.

One thing I did feel I wanted to continue was my advocacy for dogs with IVDD, and dogs in wheelchairs. I just had to figure out a way in which I'd move forward with that.

As I looked at my journal, revisiting what I'd unfolded by allowing my thoughts to freely flow, it was a relief to feel something concrete in what I *did* know.

Another interesting observation was that my days seemed to lack structure without my "to-do" lists. I had become so accustomed to setting a schedule for different tasks I needed to accomplish each day. Not having this linear list still made me feel as if I didn't have a road map of where I needed to go. At times it was unbearable and I wanted to jump right out of my skin! Why is it so hard for most human beings to just slow down and be?

Here was the gift of time right in front of me, smack dab in my lap, and I was wasting time worrying. I needed to change my thinking. I had to look at this time of contemplation and reflection as the *work* I'm meant to be doing right now.

Being curious by nature, I shifted my thinking about this as an adventure. When I did so I became more curious about what I would discover along the way during this silent excursion.

Later that evening I felt the need to go to my journal once again, but before I opened it to write, another thought popped into my head. I wanted to reread a book called *The Second Journey*. I smiled, wondering where that came from, but trusted it was for a reason.

I had learned a long time ago that these seemingly at random thoughts that appear out of nowhere are Spirit's way of guiding me. It's almost as if they were impulses that I was being challenged to follow, and not dismiss.

I walked over to my bookshelf. It didn't take me long to find the book by Joan Anderson; I had all her books and they'd become very dear to me over the years. Holding it in my hands, I slowly ran my hand over the cover. The minute I did this, I felt this wave of comfort wash over me.

As I sat back down on the sofa and opened to the first chapter I instantly felt like I was visiting a friend I'd known for a lifetime—a friend who had been through a time of inner turbulence in her own life, and someone who would be my guide as I sojourned on my continued path of solitude.

CHAPTER TWENTY

Listening Below the Noise

Joan Anderson's words were just what I needed to hear to help me feel not so alone. As I've gotten older, my belief in the divine also continues to grow stronger. I know I was guided to this book in that particular moment to provide just the right wisdom.

I now added Grace cards to my daily ritual. Created by life coach Cheryl Richardson, each of these 5 x 3 ½ – sized cards had a special message. I'd used them on and off over the years, sometimes referring to them when I had a question about a certain decision I needed to make, or oftentimes simply as inspiration or guidance. It never failed to amaze me how often I picked a card at random that seemed to have just the right message for me.

Each day, after I finished journaling, I would shuffle the cards for a few seconds, then cut the deck in half and chose the top card of the second pile.

Ask—When we call upon the Divine for guidance and support, we will receive a response. Spiritual signposts will be put in our path to guide us to our highest good.

When I got this card, goosebumps ran up and down my spine. It was certainly a confirmation that I was doing the right thing. I couldn't help but think how I had reached out to my mentor, Dan, when I was trying to make a decision about taking this sabbatical. The card spoke loud and clear to me that I was doing the right thing.

But I did wonder if we could just simply ask. While it sounds so simple, it can be a challenge. I could attest to this, as I often want to control most of what happens in my life. Asking for help isn't always easy. But there was relief in being open to spiritual signposts and that by asking for help we can be divinely guided, though I knew my head would continue to challenge me on this.

At the same time, I was beginning to understand that when we let the busy tasks of daily living swallow us up, the signs of reassurance and sense of direction can be hard to see.

After writing the message from the Grace card in my journal, many thoughts followed it onto the page. One of the many things I needed to work through was feeling like I had been constantly "on" for the past six years. Every moment of each day, including many weekends, were filled with promoting my work, fulfilling my mission, writing my books, along with day-to-day living expectations of nurturing relationships, keeping house, appointments, errands and grocery shopping.

It became quite clear I had burnt myself out. No wonder when Joie passed away I felt like I had nothing left to give. It was the truth. All my energy had been zapped from me.

Social media, while wonderful in many ways in helping me build a name for myself as a writer and animal advocate, had me in a state of feeling like I had to "do it all." It was one of the feelings I battled to push away time and time again. I believed I had to keep on top of it all.

My passion to share my message was so strong and worked in my favor. It was that drive that had allowed me to build a community of like-minded people without getting lost in the noise out there. But now I was beginning to see that it was the intense pressure I had put upon myself that had landed me right where I was now. Addressing this on the page gave it a voice and that inner part of me was feeling more satisfied in being heard.

The more difficult feeling I wrestled with was how I had been in a place of complete knowing six years before. It was a day in the summer of 2007 when I just knew, without a doubt, that I had to write a children's book about Frankie.

From that point on, I had been driven by this unseen force. Nothing was going to stop me from sharing Frankie's story. I had defined this as finding what so many seek: my purpose. But now, with Frankie gone, and Joie too, that purpose seemed to have evaporated.

I continued to journal, even when I felt dizzy from all the emotions I was addressing on each page. I knew I couldn't force any answers about where I was going next, because only time would tell. A wise voice inside me said, "Be patient." Each time I closed my journal for the day, I knew I had to continue to try and rest in this place of transition.

The next morning I was eager to pick another Grace card. I hoped it would provide another clue and a piece of wisdom. It read:

Illumination—Believe in the power of grace. When we least expect it, a new door will open and the light of grace will illuminate our next step.

I smiled to myself. How often we get caught up expecting life to go along as we planned that we don't *allow* grace to lead the way. This is especially true, I think, when we feel lost, as I currently did. While I still wanted answers now, I was being called to believe again in the unseen, instead of just jumping into something that may not be fulfilling.

I recalled how years before my life coach Diane had helped me to listen and hone in on what I truly wanted. A big revelation was when I realized I had been blaming others for the fact that I wasn't finding the joy I so desperately wanted.

At the time I was a distributor for a nutritional supplement company. I didn't realize I was doing it at the time, but I had begun to find fault with one person or another and how I didn't think they were doing their part in helping us grow as a team.

The truth was I had been ignoring that little voice inside me, trying to tell me that this opportunity just wasn't for me. I remember being afraid to admit it this to myself because I thought it would mean I was a failure. But I'd also come to realize that no one else was responsible for my joy, just me.

I had been scared and unhappy for financial reasons when I jumped into being a distributor. It wasn't fulfilling in any sense of the word, but I didn't know what else to do. It was only after coaching with Diane, which led me to become a writer about the human-animal bond, that spiritual signposts started to pop up left and right. It was an incredible time of which I felt that every step of my life was being divinely guided.

Recalling all of this now was a reminder of how it was important to take this time to tune in and listen. While I didn't have a life coach guiding me, I did have the tools she'd helped me put in place years before. Patience has not always been my strong suit, but although I was eager to feel that same bliss I'd felt for six years while working with Frankie, I knew I had to be still, listen, and accept the fact that my next step would reveal itself in due time.

Just the night before I had read these wise words in *The Second Journey:* "You must literally be willing to begin again and again…energy is generated in the tension, the struggle…the pull and tug is everything."

While in one way it felt heavy and I was exhausted at the thought of beginning yet again, another part of me was excited about new possibilities. Even though the "tug and pull" felt a bit overwhelming, it also made perfect sense.

I understand that I must be willing to move through these times of feeling uncertain and in somewhat unchartered territory. It meant letting go of what was and accepting my days to now unfold in a natural rhythm. It was my job to find a way in which to rest in this place of trusting.

For now, this helped the fear monster retreat to a safe place. I was right where I was supposed to be for this time frame in my life. But I did wonder how often I was going to have to remind myself of this. The back and forth in my mind could be awfully tiring.

But the more I wrote, working through all my myriad of feelings, the more comfortable I was becoming. I also began to see a glimpse of this time as a gift of exploration.

Digging through my files, I found the navy blue folder I'd kept from my sessions with Diane. They contained the notes I'd taken, along with exercises she'd given me to help assess different parts of my life.

One exercise was to write a list of ideas that were of interest to me. It ended up to be quite a long list because there were so many things I was interested in! But part of the process was to narrow it down and find one area of interest to explore deeper. I recalled how agonizing this was for me. I couldn't believe I could only pick one, and every fiber of my being tried to rebel against it.

Now, as I looked through the list, I was transported back in time.

- Work part-time at a library or bookstore.
- Become a developer with John, building small, cottage-style homes.

- Start a dog walking business.
- Work at a floral shop.
- Become a pet massage therapist.
- Volunteer at a nursing home and hospital with my dog.
- Learn animal communication.
- Become a writer.

While I had ultimately chosen to become a writer, I now realized I'd also become a volunteer at a nursing home and hospital. I remembered hoping it would be Kylie who worked as a therapy dog, but oh how the road had taken a different turn.

Revisiting this, I realized how much I had accomplished since Diane's coaching. Everything had worked out and unfolded in such a beautiful way. From being a volunteer, it naturally flowed into my writing life. I wrote many posts on my blog about the experience. It also led to a second children's book about Frankie's visits to a senior assisted living facility, Libby's House. Three years later this led to the writing and publishing of *Through Frankie's Eyes*.

This journey now served as proof that while I'd been in this inbetween place before, I was eventually led to a fulfilling time in my life.

I read over the list one more time, and this time what jumped out at me was animal communication. Oddly enough, I didn't remember writing that or having that interest at the time.

It made the hairs on my arms stand up because I had recently written in my journal that I wanted to host a workshop in my home with my friend, author and animal communicator, Dawn Brunke.

I remembered the day I had to put Joie to sleep and the distraught email I'd sent Dawn. Her kind and compassionate response was that I could call her if I needed to. I took her up on it that evening. It wasn't an actual reading with Joie, but rather a friend reaching out to a friend in a time of need.

Dawn, being so tuned in with animals, did sense Joie with us as we talked. While Joie was, for the most part quiet, there was one thing that Dawn conveyed to me that was coming through loud and clear. Joie wanted me to understand that this time since her passing was a time for me to just *be* and to let go of *doing* so much.

Another message came through, one that was hard for me to hear. Joie "told" Dawn that I no longer needed to prove myself. My throat immediately tightened and hot tears filled my eyes. She struck a painful chord.

While she was right, I knew it would take me time to work through this. Feeling unworthy was something I'd carried around for a long time, though I really had no idea where it came from.

I was grateful for Dawn's insight, even though I felt drained afterward. We said our goodbyes and I knew I'd need to be gentle with myself as I worked through these messages from Joie.

CHAPTER TWENTY-ONE

Grace Leads the Way

A few days after my phone conversation with Dawn, my friend Mary sent me the following quote: *He came into the quiet of his life. The bear inside was sleeping.*

Mary told me it was from the movie, *Legends of the Fall.* The film is narrated by an older Native American man who imparts much wisdom to Tristan, the main character, who was played by Brad Pitt. The quote referred to a period of transition in his life and it reminded Mary of me.

"For so long," she said, "you have been on this going-all-the-time treadmill and all you've done with Frankie and Joie. And at the same time, your writing and inner work seem to be heading in the opposite direction."

While I'd never seen the movie, the quote gave me goosebumps. I saw it as another confirmation from Spirit to keep following this path of stillness and rumination.

Riding the wave of synchronicity, I pulled a Grace card. I almost couldn't believe my eyes when I read the card.

> *Self—Go within. When we invest more energy in devel-oping our Spiritual lives, the outer world begins to take care of itself.*

I had to marvel at this one. Oftentimes it took several signs—or as I liked to say, a two-by-four to the head—for me to see things clearly. "Okay, Universe!" I said aloud, "I hear you loud and clear."

There was no denying that this quest was about self-care and something I needed to trust and follow through on. I couldn't second guess myself or worry what others may think. I *had* to do this for me. It was just like when I made the decision to hire a life coach; I vividly remember telling myself that if I took this time just for me, I would come out the other side a better person.

While I felt I'd made a huge leap in my consciousness, Spirit still had more to bring to my attention. This became obvious as I read more of Joan Anderson's *The Second Journey* that evening.

Lately, I find myself being pulled toward Spirit, beginning to sense that the second half of life is meant to be more internal than external—a time for feeling and less thinking.

Relying heavily on the work of Joseph Campbell, Anderson went on to say that a self-imposed pilgrimage is a quest, one where you might not know what you're looking for, but you have acknowledged that you're looking for something.

"If you are ready," Campbell had said, "then the doors will open where there were no doors and here will come aids, as well as difficult trials."

I certainly felt that pull to live from that internal place Joan spoke of. But I couldn't help but think how many struggle with going inward, at least in part because of how society defines success by the amount of money we make and the possessions we accumulate. But what about the person who lives contently within their own self-worth and defining a meaningful life as such? So many are seeking this, but as a society we don't place much value on it. Campbell and Anderson's philosophies were definitely in line with my own in terms of how I could find my way back to renewing my sense of Spirit and self. In particular, Campbell's insistence that the pilgrim had to give up something really hit home.

As I let Joan's thought sink deeper into my consciousness, I did realize that the last few days of my sabbatical I could actually hear myself thinking and moving through feeling all the different facets of emotions. I had also made the decision to limit my exposure to my cell phone and my computer. I could clearly feel the difference in my energy levels now that they weren't being zapped by my electronics.

It was intriguing, to say the least, to be an observer of my thought patterns. One day I would feel I knew for sure what this thing called life was all about, only to find myself going down the path of worrying the next. But I'd gently remind myself this is the process and the *work*. My job wasn't to figure out anything right now, but to just be in a state of compassionate observance.

One challenge I observed as I journaled was addressing my need to feel like I had to find that next thing to *do*. Did I have a fear of life passing me by? Was there a sense of urgency to reach some sort of defined "top"? Did I feel pressured by others or by society? What exactly was it? These were the issues I needed to work through.

While I was beginning to feel more grounded, I also knew I needed to linger in this quiet space of nothingness for however long it took—even when the voices from the outside world or my inner critic were trying to convince me otherwise.

The late Dr. Wayne Dyer, who I had always considered a mentor, referred to cultural beliefs and how we've bought into them as "memes." A meme is defined as "an element of a culture or system of behavior that may be considered to be passed from one individual to another by non-genetic means, especially imitation."

Dyer seemed to be suggesting that we had lost the ability to really think for ourselves. Instead of taking the time to really be with our minds, many of us just bought into what the rest of the world is doing.

One thing I knew for sure was I wanted to honor this gift that was now here for me because of Joie's unexpected passing. To not honor this time of *being* just for me, even though the outside world may balk at it, I felt like I would be dishonoring Joie's existence. I couldn't let that happen.

Acknowledging this helped me shift deeper into another level of acceptance—the acceptance of being okay with what was right for *my* life, regardless of what someone else may say is best for me. Joie's presence in Spirit also helped me to not feel alone. All I needed to do to be with her and her teachings was to sit in silence and invite her into that sacred space, and know that we are all truly connected.

I lingered for a few moments longer, processing everything that came into my awareness today. It was fascinating, watching my mind and seeing where it went. And I smiled as a word popped into my head that seemed to perfectly define this place of being and what it was all about—I was *marinating*. All these ideas, thoughts, observations, and exploration could be summed up as just that.

Marinating was a way of letting it all co-mingle in my mind, giving each part of me and my thought process time to be heard. The more I did this and acknowledged my inner world, the more peaceful moments I was beginning to experience.

CHAPTER TWENTY-TWO

A Sign from Joie

That Friday evening John, Nikki and I gathered around the chiminea to relax and end the week with an adult beverage.

John and Nikki were quiet, lost in their own thoughts gazing into the glowing embers of the fire, while I finished reading another chapter in *The Second Journey*. I read a passage that made tears immediately spring to my eyes because I knew it to be the truth of what I needed to hear and understand.

Nothing happens overnight. Developing a relationship with the unknown takes time. In doing so the seeker is granted the greatest gift of all—clarity. I have come full circle yet again. I must always be willing to journey forward—spiral into the center and then back out again. Then and only then will I be whole, in touch with all that I am.

I read it again because I really wanted to soak it deep into my being.

"Wow."

"What's wow?" Nikki said, startling me from my thoughts. I hadn't realized I'd spoken aloud.

I looked at her and John, who was now looking at me too.

"Can I share with you what I just read?"

At their nods of encouragement, I began reading the passage, my throat tightening with emotion.

"I'm exactly where I need to be right now," I said with recognition and a touch of apprehension. While I still didn't know what was next for me, I understood this as part of my journey to be necessary in order to help lead me in the right direction.

"Yup, I think so, too," Nikki said, and although her tone was casual, I knew she understood the deeper meaning.

It felt as if I was suspended in time as I digested this piece of wisdom from Anderson. In somewhat of a daze, I picked up the drink sitting on the arm of my Adirondack chair and took a sip.

It was humid that evening so condensation had formed on my glass. Still holding it in my hand, I glanced down at the arm of my chair and what I saw took my breath away!

Droplets of water had dripped onto the arm of the chair in the perfect shape of a paw print. For a brief moment I thought perhaps my eyes were playing a trick on me.

But then I knew…I just *knew* it was a message from Joie, reminding me to continue taking time for myself. She was reassuring me that I was on the right path. The hairs on my arms stood on end.

Pointing to the water print, I said, "John and Nikki, look! It's a sign from Joie!"

"Oh my gosh," Nikki exclaimed, "I have goosebumps!"

When I looked at John his mouth was hanging open in amazement. "Wow, I think you are right."

"I *know* I'm right. I can *feel* it. It's Joie. She's assuring me that I'm right where I'm supposed to be."

"You have to take a picture!" Nikki said.

Grateful for her quick thinking, I hurried to my writing cottage and grabbed my camera. I still look at the photo to this day and am so glad I have it when I have doubts. In fact, if you take a moment to look now, it's the paw print you see on the cover of this book behind the word pause.

Nikki, whom I had told about the Grace cards, asked, "What card did you pick today?"

I flipped to the day's journal entry and read,

Inspire—to breathe life into what is true.

In almost perfect unison we each began rubbing our hands up and down our arms because they were covered with goosebumps. I believed with all my heart the paw print was Joie's way of breathing life into what I had been feeling but didn't know how to express. It was proof to me that those who have passed over, whether human or pet, are here with us and will guide us if we are open to receiving their help. Observing Joie's presence in the watery paw print made me come alive in a way I didn't expect. While I still didn't know what the near future held for me, I now felt more comfortable and at peace accepting where I was right now and that not having answers was okay. The sign also reminded me that the Universe was supporting me and that when we trust in Spirit, miracles will show up.

The next day I started to look more into animal communication and soon found myself compiling a list of articles and books on the subject.

While I'd never really tried to just sit and listen for messages from my dogs, I'd certainly had my share of interesting signs from them—signs that were too hard to just brush aside as coincidental. I've always believed when these signs occurred in my life that they were real. They also always seemed to serve a purpose in guiding me in some shape or form. They either helped to heal me on some level, or helped to strengthen what I already knew and felt inside me. I recalled talking with a friend whose dog had passed away a few months ago and how she knew in her heart she got a sign from him that he was okay on the other side.

She said, "Barb, I'm sure Snoopy came to me as a firefly."

I know there are many that would question the validity of this—not to mention my friend's sanity—but I believe strongly that our loved ones find ways to let us know they are safe and still here, just in a different form. When we trust in these moments of connection, it brings us indescribable feelings of joy and peace.

"If that is what you felt in your heart," I told her, "then it *is* real."

The thoughts and emotions were coming so strong and fast that morning I couldn't seem to write them fast enough in my journal. My hand flew across the page as I tried to capture them all, knowing that they would help me to become stronger in what I truly believe but am sometimes afraid to voice out loud.

When I was finally finished, I closed my journal and turned to the Grace cards lying next to me. Shuffling them a card jumped from the deck:

> *Strength—Face your fear. Every challenge is a blessing in disguise, a gift that makes us stronger, more conscious and ultimately, more alive.*

I chuckled softly and wondered if I had a direct line to Spirit. Once again, the Grace card I chose seemed to say exactly what I needed to hear for the day.

This made me think about one of my fears, which is that others will think I'm a bit "out there" for believing we can communicate with animals and that we can receive signs from them. I took a few moments to acknowledge these feelings.

As I sat in this space of looking at my fear, but paying more attention to how I've felt in those moments of connection, I realized how they've lit a fire of knowing in me when they've occurred. And each and every time I've experienced a sign from a pet from the other side, or felt a shared connection of understanding, my heart has filled with a love that I can only describe as pure.

And when these moments have happened I felt more alive. It was definitely something I knew I wanted more of and what my sabbatical was teaching me. I knew I wanted to live even more in awareness of each day and appreciate the simple joy of life.

I re-read the Grace card a few more times so it would sink deeply into every part of my being.

While in one way Joie's death felt premature, I was beginning to understand it was divine timing. What I had learned from Frankie, and what I had shared with others, was that we have to look for the blessings in every situation that we find challenging.

It was now becoming clearer to me that the blessing of Joie leaving when she did was that it led me to take this journey inward. If she was still alive, I was pretty sure I would not have done so. That is not to say of course that I did not find her loss deeply painful. Once again, I took comfort in Anderson's wisdom:

> *Life is always being reconfigured. The sooner we can embrace change, the less we will struggle.*

While this thought brought up a very common fear of change, I also knew from my own experiences that when things remain the same, I don't grow.

I let Joan's advice seep into my subconscious as a guide to keep me on this path of seeing the blessings in life's detours. I understood that if we can see these forks in the road as teaching moments, it can help us to navigate the twists and turns a bit easier.

Something else in Anderson' book also resonated. She suggests that we strive to go deeper, rather than just forward and cautions us "to be aware of speed as it is often one's undoing."

Oh, how I could relate! I was on this fast track, believing that it was how I was *supposed* to be. In this, too, I am hardly unique—it is ingrained in our culture.

But, as my writing revealed, my soul had been craving this quieter, deeper place. It was there in every line of every page. But I didn't consciously realize it because I was too busy trying to juggle all the many things on my plate. But now I could no longer ignore the message my inner self was giving me:

I was in transition, and had been ever since Frankie passed. I hadn't wanted to let go of her or the work we did because it had become such a big part of my identity.

But I was now ready to acknowledge that subconsciously I was trying to have Joie fill the void Frankie had left. All the while I'd been hearing the whisper to let that chapter close and start on a new path, but it had been too scary to face the unknown at the time.

The Second Journey also advises us to "let go of what is outlived to make room for the unlived." When I read this for the first time I actually let out a small gasp, then wrote it down in my journal so I wouldn't forget. As I continued through my sabbatical I found myself revisiting this quote often and mulling it around in my mind.

I also found myself contemplating her use of the term "unfinished women." The first time I read this, it felt like a negative assessment; now, however, it made more sense. I take it as meaning we have the opportunity to explore all the many different facets of ourselves and that we have many opportunities along the way to become better versions of ourselves. These moments, I've found, oftentimes nudge us more strongly during a time of change.

I also began asking the questions I'd not given thought to in quite some time, such as "Why am I here?" "What is my purpose?" Honestly, this was a place I hadn't expected to find myself in again. I thought I'd answered that question when I found my purpose had been fulfilled with the books I'd written about Frankie and how I took great joy in sharing her story with so many. But when she died everything came to a sudden halt. I was left questioning whether we get the chance to have more than one purpose.

If so, how do we go about finding it?

While at times it was difficult to face all these different swirls of emotions vying for my attention, I kept going back to Joan Anderson's observation that we are unfinished women. It helped me to continue this phase of exploration that I could expand deeper into who I already was. In doing so I would be led to what was next.

Getting to this broader point of understanding and consciousness helped me feel closer to the center of peace I was seeking. I was beginning to understand that the more shadowy parts of myself that played out as fear actually served a purpose too in that they are here to protect me. I just needed to make sure that I gave them their due attention and satisfied their need to be heard.

CHAPTER TWENTY-THREE

Learning to *Be*

As fascinating as it was to be paying attention to all my different thought patterns, it was much more important to discern which thoughts were truly mine and which were those I'd been conditioned to believe.

As Nikki moved into an apartment of her own, I found myself experiencing some twinges of envy. She now had all this time in the world to explore everything that's important to her with no concerns about anyone else's needs. I had married John right out of college and while I had no regrets about that decision, I still had those occasional "what if" moments.

On the other hand, Nikki served as a reminder of what I didn't want any longer. She was constantly on the go—just thinking about the ladder she was climbing left me feeling exhausted! Observing this, I realized that slowing down was right where I wanted to be at this time in my life. My former need to be "in the spotlight" was waning, and my inner journey and savoring the simple pleasures was more appealing than ever.

As the days unfolded one into another, I fully embraced this time of pausing, listening and capturing what was now important to me. Fall was now in full bloom with cooler nights, and snuggling on the sofa, lost in a good book. It was bliss.

Well almost. There was one thing missing that continued to tug on my heart. With winter approaching, I couldn't bear to think of going through the snowy, cold months without another dachshund as a faithful and loyal companion. The two just seemed to go together for me.

John was also planning on installing a woodstove in our living room when we returned from our vacation in mid-October. It was something we had dreamed about ever since we rented that cabin in Vermont the previous year. We had so enjoyed gathering around the burning embers each evening to talk about our day's adventures, and now we wanted to replicate this feeling in our own home. Of course in my mind, a dachshund was part of this cozy scene.

While I knew I wanted to open my heart and my home to another special needs doxie, I didn't feel the sense of urgency I'd had when adopting Joie. My heart was still healing on many different levels. I didn't want to jump too fast into getting another dog. It was comforting for now that I was giving thought to another pup but could wait until the time was right.

This time I also decided I wouldn't put any stipulations around what color or age my next dachshund would be like I had done when I was looking for Joie. I just sat in sweet moments of imagination, with my new friend curled up in front of a warm, glowing woodstove with me.

One evening as I sat alone in the living room, I glanced at the wall across from me. Dubbed my "wall of love," it had a family photo of me, John, Kylie, and Frankie; a painting done by a local artist of Cassie Jo; and a painting of Frankie, done by another local artist. Finally, there was a photo I loved of Kylie and Frankie snuggling on our bed.

I got lost in all the sweet memories of life with my dogs and John. But then I realized something was missing. Tears sprang to my eyes as I realized I didn't have a photo of Joie. This felt odd, as if she had never existed. But I knew I'd never forget her despite our very short time together.

Frankie had been so visible in the public eye, and for a time I thought it was what I wanted for Joie. Of course, it hadn't turned out that way, and it was a strange feeling that others hadn't come to know Joie like they did Frankie.

Suddenly, I had this impulse to review my notes from my conversation with Dawn on the evening of Joie's death. Although Dawn wasn't giving me an official reading, just helping a grieving friend, she provided some valuable insight.

I had shared with her that I was struggling greatly with the "why" of Joie dying so soon after I adopted her. Reading my notes again, it all came rushing back to me.

Dawn was immediately able to sense Joie with us. Although Joie's energy wasn't all that strong, she did have something she wanted me to know. She wanted me to rest now and not think or worry so much anymore. Then Dawn added, "Joie is telling me to let you know that there is nothing for you to make sense of right now."

Ironically, I had a hard time understanding what that meant!

"Remember Joie," Dawn said, "is to remember all the joy and the gifts she brought you."

As I continued to read through my notes, a big teaching I hadn't seen before now jumped off the page: *I didn't need to prove anything to anyone any longer.* Joie wanted me to know I am worthy in just being alive. That no matter what things may seem like on the "outside" and no matter how many books I publish or whatever it is that I continue to do, right now it was more important to learn to just *be*.

This state of *being*, and all that it meant, was still hard for me to wrap my mind around. It was going to take time and practice. But reading my notes again helped me move to yet another level of awareness and what self-discovery is all about.

I made a mental note to find a favorite picture of Joie the next day so I could add it to my "wall of love" to help serve as a reminder of all she taught me.

Before heading to bed I shuffled my deck of Grace cards, picking one at random. It read:

Mindfulness—manage your mind. When we direct our thoughts and words toward the outcome we most desire, we ignite grace.

I quietly laughed. I knew I was most definitely a work in progress on this one. And again, I was in complete awe of how the cards had this spiritual magic about them; it was as if they were guided by some unseen source to reveal just what I need to hear to carry me forth on my journey.

My heart felt light as a feather as I thought about this new way of being. I wanted to continue to open in new ways and pay attention to what is around me, but to also trust in what I couldn't see. There is something bigger than me, guiding me at all times and had me curious about the next leg of my journey.

The following morning, sitting in my writing cottage, I heard the school bus rumble by. There was always a flurry of activity early in the morning during the school year as the neighborhood kids poured out of their houses. I loved seeing the kids in their new outfits and backpacks, chattering away as they walked to the bus stop. A few minutes later, though, I watched the bus chug down the street and realized I relished the quiet that fell over our neighborhood once they were gone.

It made me think about my many first days of school, how I loved how every year was a fresh start. It suddenly occurred to me that this was what I was experiencing right now.

Like the kids not knowing what they would learn in their new year of school, I was reminded that clarity would come for me as I opened myself to just letting each day unfold as it was meant to. In this time of transition I had the gift of reflecting on lessons learned and new adventures waiting out there for me.

When I began my sabbatical there were moments I felt like I was going to vibrate right out of my skin because so much of my time had been spent ruminating on what was next. But I was beginning to find joy in simple tasks that really didn't involve much thinking at all. I realized just how much my brain had been on overdrive in many ways these past few years!

I was enjoying household chores like cleaning out drawers, closets and files, which before seemed a heavy burden but now felt like moments of Zen. Functions like throwing in a load of laundry, stacking dishes in the dishwasher or tidying up around the house made me feel grounded.

My home has always been important to me. It's my foundation and the safe place I can be surrounded by my dogs and the love of John. It made me appreciate all that I had even more. I thought about the many times John came home and said, "You make our home so cozy." It's a compliment I've never tired of and take great pride in.

Thinking about our home and how I wanted to continue to live from the truth of who I am brought something to the forefront of my mind. Like many people in our fast-paced, high-tech world, I'd asked myself this more than once. "How does one balance it all?"

Now, even as I found myself in this blessed place of slowing down, I had this niggle that didn't want to completely let go either. One day soon I would want to find something that would honor and feed my soul on a deeper level.

Finding balance is something I've often heard other women talking about, and have even had this conversation with many friends.

It seems we have gotten to a point of wanting it *all*, from taking care of our homes and family, to doing work that is meaningful, and taking time for ourselves.

But how could we possibly balance all of that? It seems one thing or another will suffer in the process; at least this is the conclusion I was heavily leaning toward.

While I had been busy pursuing my passion and trying to keep up with everything else, I was pushing away an inner whisper that wanted desperately to be acknowledged—the urge to slow down and not try and do so much.

I've come to think that perhaps there really is no such thing as balance. And this is where I hold my hand up and confess, "I can't do it all." Maybe there is a time for everything we wish to pursue, but just not all at once. Perhaps we have to pursue each task or intention in smaller chunks of time.

The question of balance went round and round in my mind like a hamster on a wheel, even as my hand tried to capture these thoughts in my journal. Finally, I grew tired of trying to figure out an answer and gently shut the cover. The question would still be there tomorrow, and the day after that.

I have since resigned myself to the fact that there is no definitive answer to this balance question. We each must continue to experiment with what is right for us individually and our own circumstances. Most importantly, we must look deeper when we feel out of step, rather than just assuming it's because we don't have enough time for ourselves. There may be something bigger going on.

With my mind exhausted from diving deep in search of answers, I decided a mundane task was in order. And there is nothing more mundane, I think, than cleaning out office files.

Truth be told, I was curious as to what cleaning out the old would do in terms of eventually bringing in new creative avenues that I trusted were already on their way to me. In the past when tossing out what no longer served me, I was always amazed at the new visionary energy that was allowed to come in.

As I began cleaning out my files, I was more convinced than ever that this was no menial task. My mind was trying to tell me that I should be doing something that mattered more. This called for a Grace card to intercept. It read:

Surrender—surrender is the key that unlocks the door to grace.

Shaking my head back and forth, I said out loud, "Okay! Okay!" as I looked up to the ceiling addressing the big Spirit in the universe, "I get it! I get it!" I shall surrender to this moment of not worrying or thinking I should be doing more. I will trust that grace is leading the way.

CHAPTER TWENTY-FOUR

Moving Toward Clarity

The next morning as I tried to just go with the flow of the day, it felt like a heap of Mexican jumping beans were having a party inside my stomach. Here I was again in this distressing place of trying to stay in a space of stillness and quiet. I was upset that just when I'd make progress in acceptance that this was right where I needed to be, I'd be filled with doubt and take two steps back.

Why was it that for so long I'd been craving this time alone and now that it was here I was having these moments of wanting to run the other way? Can't I just be happy with what *is*, I wondered? I was frustrated. Part of the reason is that I felt odd. I didn't want to strive toward some goal or achievement— at least for now.

I wondered though about others who feel their life is too hectic but are too afraid to stop long enough to give thought to what it is they really want. I'd certainly read enough self-help books and listened to enough Hay House Radio to know this is something many struggle with. But it is fear that stops many from listening to what their soul may be trying to convey to them.

It's when we sit still long enough to tune in to that inner world of truth that looms large and feels too scary to address.

At least it was the case for me. What if I didn't like what my heart was trying to tell me? What if what I truly wanted was different from others?

But one thing I knew right in this very moment was that I had to accept this restless feeling. I had to understand I wasn't in control. And there it was again—the one thing that we humans keep trying to accomplish—trying to control some unforeseen outcome that may never even happen. I silently said, *Repeat after me, Barb. You. Are. Not. In. Control.*

Grabbing my journal, I wrote my way through the uneasy feelings this conjured up. Seeing my thoughts on the page validated those feelings and at the same time helped me understand that they were just thoughts run amuck. Oh, what a reminder of how powerful our minds can be!

By allowing my thoughts to have a voice on the page, for the moment, helped lighten the load my head was trying desperately to make sense of everything. It also helped me to feel safe and allowed my spirit to move another step closer to a peace within.

In many ways this process is how I feel about grieving, and that we have to give ourselves the room to move through, and within it, at our own pace. There is no right or wrong way to grieve and there is no magic formula to make it easier. Being in this place of unanswered questions, trying to understand the next step to take, I knew this is what I had to do now, too. If I sat long enough with the uncomfortable feelings they would eventually pass or find a soft place to land. Clarity was only going to be found if I continued to feel my way through.

This time of grieving and not pushing forward was, in fact, my purpose now. I began to really sense that if I stayed the course of this inner traveling my path would continue to reveal the next steps for me.

Before closing my journal for yet another day, I completed the daily ritual I was coming to really enjoy by choosing a Grace card. It read:

Silence—be still. A daily practice of silence bears gifts— a heightened sensitivity to beauty, deep inner peace, and a profound feeling of connectedness to all living things.

Perhaps by now, dear readers, you might find it hard to believe that every time I picked a card it aligned with the truth of where I was in the moment. And believe me, I was finding it hard to believe, too. At times I thought my eyes were playing tricks on me! And I had to read the card I chose today twice to let it sink in.

I wanted to get the message and take it deeply in, as if my life depended on it. And in a way, it did. If I wanted to move forward, this was clearly a sign of what I had to do if I wanted to discover what was in store for me next. It was everything I'd just been thinking about and the cards picked up on my energy!

All this intense thinking reminded me of something well-meaning folks have told me at one time or another, and that is that I sometimes think too much! I knew they intended no harm, yet there have been times when I've taken that remark as a negative, and it stung.

But as my days in reflection and contemplation unfolded, I realized that this is what makes me, *me*. For the most part, thinking deeply is like trying to solve a puzzle—the puzzle being myself and what it is that makes me tick, how I see the world around me, and then learning to navigate within it that feels right for me.

Being in the "think tank" helps me put the pieces of what I call me together in a way that helps me see myself more fully. While there are times when I had this absolute knowing I was right where I was supposed to be, I was beginning to understand that other times, such as I was experiencing now, were just as important pieces to the puzzle.

This piece of the puzzle was now in the right place, which was accepting that pondering one's life *is* part of the puzzle in order for us to journey forward in the best way.

My life's path over the past six years had absolutely felt divinely orchestrated and even though a part of me wanted so badly to feel that certainty again, I knew now that being in this suspended space of unknown was only temporary.

While I knew I was jumping here, there, and everywhere on the page of my journal, I didn't judge my thoughts. I just let them emerge so they didn't stay stuck inside. And after a myriad of scattered thoughts I suddenly wrote on the page, "I need to reach out to my friend, Diane."

This had been on my list I had put together when I began my sabbatical. It was as if the universe was saying that it was now the right time to follow through. She had always had a way of helping me see every side of myself, and now my spirit soared just thinking about sitting down with her for a heart-to-heart. This small glimpse into clarity seemed to leave as fast as it came. I gazed out my writing cottage window, and stared past the pine trees in the neighbor's yard as I tried to figure out this hollow feeling of emptiness. It seemed to have come out of nowhere after feeling so sure of what I wanted to do next.

Where was this empty feeling coming from? And then Frankie popped into my mind, and I felt this pang in my heart. Trying not to judge it, I just sat with the feeling. It was then that I realized what this feeling was. For so long I had felt her spirit strongly whenever I spent time in my writing cottage, which was most days, for a good part of the day. But almost like a light that switched off, I knew in that moment she was no longer here. Something had shifted within the room. I clearly sensed her presence had moved on in that moment.

I recognized it in part as why this hollow feeling in the pit of my stomach came over me, while at the same time I was happy for her. She was on her way now, transitioning to wherever it was that would bring her joy. While my heart ached in one sense, in another it became a sweet moment of understanding that I too, would find my own way through this current transition.

Those moments felt like I was suspended in another realm. And I knew that the greatest gift I could give Frankie was acknowledging I was okay with her moving on to a deeper place of rest. By doing so, I felt a shift of a new space opening within me. For so long, that space had been taken up by holding Frankie so close to me, afraid to let go.

I don't know how long I sat there, but it was a pivotal shift that needed to happen. I was grateful for it. Slowly, I began to feel my body back in my chair and I was focusing again on the trees outside my window. I grabbed my Grace cards, shuffled them and turned one over.

Awaken—Keep your eyes open. When we decide to live a more conscious life, we see signs of grace everywhere.

After writing the quote in my journal I was compelled to write down this thought: "I want to live a more conscious life. I want less hustle and bustle. I want deeper conversations and more meaningful moments."

The following day I had plans with a friend I'd lost touch with. We'd been in each other's lives years before, but then drifted apart. She lives in the same town and of late we were bumping into each other at local restaurants or the post office. While our town is small, I couldn't help but think that synchronicity was at work because before this it was rare we'd run into one another by chance.

I'd been simmering in the idea of finding a way in which I could encourage women—women just like me who have felt lost or unsure at times in their lives—and perhaps were looking for a sense of purpose and meaning.

My friend, Shannon, now in her mid-forties, was someone I knew was giving thought to what her life would look like when her two kids went off to college.

We sat at a small table, near the back of a dimly lit restaurant as I shared my thoughts about how I wanted to find a way to encourage other women to take time to listen to their hearts and pursue what is important to them. Though I told her I really didn't know what that looked like or how I could be of service in that way.

I said, "I'm thinking that maybe I'd like to offer workshops for women who are in transition, and giving thought to what is perhaps next for their lives. I'm curious your thoughts on this."

Just as the last words came out of my mouth, it was obvious I'd struck a chord. Shannon's eyes filled with tears and they began rolling down her cheeks.

It was hard for her to talk. She finally managed to slowly eek out, "I'm sorry...I'm so emotional about this...I don't know why."

I put my hand on her forearm. "It's okay, take your time. It seems meant to be that I asked you this question."

She nodded as she took a few deep breaths. "There is this light about you. It's why I like to be around you."

Now my eyes filled with tears. It was such a lovely compliment. "Wow, thank you. I'm honored you said this."

While I'd had others tell me I have this positive energy about me, to hear Shannon describe it as a light, and why she liked being around me, was very touching.

She told me what she had recently shared with her husband Bradd after having dinner with me and John two weeks earlier. "I mentioned to Bradd that I felt your light wasn't as bright anymore. I wondered what may be wrong."

I knew what she meant. It was what I'd been trying to work through for quite some time. I'd certainly felt like my sparkle had faded. It was a big part of the reason I was taking this time for a sabbatical to try and figure out how to get it back.

"Well, I think a part of it is because of losing Joie so suddenly. But I also just feel a little lost right now. I'm not sure what I'm supposed to do next with my life. It feels odd because for the last six years I thought I had it all figured out."

Shannon nodded. She shared with me how she loves her husband and her two kids, but that something was missing for her. She didn't know exactly what it is. "I just want to be happy," she said.

She told me about some of her dreams and how she thought maybe she could start pursuing something that mattered to *her*—something just for her now that her daughter was going off to college, and her son would be graduating from high school in two years.

What she was sharing with me wasn't something new. I'd heard this countless times from other women and having read about this in self-help books. Even though I'd never had children, I'd gone through this soul searching myself in my early forties. And now here I was again, in many ways, caught off guard and in search mode.

Spending time with Shannon, talking about our thoughts and dreams gave me the courage to explore my ideas further. It was also a confirmation that time with my life coach, and friend, Diane would be a good place to start to help sort this out and receive insightful guidance.

Later that day, I thought about that light Shannon described that she saw in me. I knew it meant so much to me to be a positive figure in the world. I'd certainly been that for Nikki. And though challenging at times, it was rewarding and such a gift to be a mentor to her.

That evening I found myself pulling Sue Monk Kidd's *When the Heart Waits* off my bookshelf. I hadn't read it in years, yet suddenly it was calling out to me.

As I opened the cover and opened to a page at random, a paragraph grabbed my attention.

We're born on one level, only to find some new struggle toward wholeness gestating within. That is the sacred intent of life, of God—to move us continually toward growth, toward recovering all that is lost and orphaned within us and restoring the divine image imprinted on our soul. And rarely do significant shifts come without a sense of being lost in dark woods, or in what T.S. Elliot called, the vacant interstellar space.

A shiver ran down my spine. This described to a tee what I was feeling. This was another wonderful nugget of insight that this process of "being lost in the woods" is an important piece of the puzzle that helps us to continue to grow and heal. To see the words on the page in this way was yet more evidence, and a relief in many ways, that yes, this is how life works.

I opened my journal and poured my heart onto the page. I wrote about how I didn't like feeling sad. The departure of both Nikki and Joie had left a heaviness that I wasn't quite sure how to process.

But even though I didn't know quite sure how to move forward, I understood I had to ride these waves of emotions; this is what grief is—what life is, really. There are no promises that this time on earth is going to be a smooth ride—the ups and downs are what make life what it *is*.

This uncertainty, if I continued to trust it, would lead to clarity. While I felt convinced of this at times, it was when low moments overtook me, that I wrestled on and off with more times than I cared to count, when doubt overshadowed everything. But each moment of uncertainty was a test to lean back into trusting what I could not yet see was on its way.

As I continued to work through my feelings on the page, it suddenly felt as though my pen was taken over by the divine. I wrote, "I still want to write." This brought me joy and a huge sense of relief. I'd been scared when I began this time away, feeling a hollow void inside, that perhaps I may never want to write again. I knew the statement meant writing for my blog again at some point and possibly future books, and not just personal journaling.

I stared off into space and found myself day dreaming, imagining a dachshund curled up in a bed in my writing cottage. She would be my writing muse and my friend. She wouldn't be in the lime light like Frankie had been, or what I thought I wanted Joie to be. I really just wanted her all to myself.

After I closed my journal I picked up the Grace cards and shuffled them. It was late and I thought it would be lovely to have a message as something to ponder as I headed to bed for the night. A card that had presented itself once before, showed up again.

Surrender—surrender is the key that unlocks the door to grace.

As I lay in bed, I found myself deepening into the meaning of surrender. While at times it certainly has been difficult, I was grasping that if I could continue to find the courage to let go, that yes, this is when grace will find me and grant me peace once again. I was living into this little by little each day as I sat in stillness, learning to gently let go of how I *thought* my life should be and instead being open to the mystery.

CHAPTER TWENTY-FIVE

Spiritual Signposts

The next morning, two thoughts were sitting on the edge of my mind begging to be written in my journal, which these days, was never out of reach. Before even getting out of bed I grabbed it from my nightstand and opened it. "I want to live a simpler and quieter life," I wrote, "and I want to understand all animals on a deeper level." While I'd contemplated these thoughts before it was now obvious how much these things mattered to me. By capturing them on paper, I saw them repeating and they were becoming like affirmations.

After getting those pressing thoughts down on paper, I got out of bed and opened the blinds on the French patio doors. Five sparrows were flitting about the bird bath perched on the top of the deck railing near my writing cottage. They drew me in as I sat on the edge of my bed. I felt called to just be in this space with them.

Two of the sparrows jumped into the water and began splashing about while two others leaned over the edge to carefully take a sip of water. The fifth bird acted like what appeared to be the lookout captain, making sure the other birds were safe.

Two other species of birds that I wasn't familiar with swooped in toward the bird bath and then back out to a nearby tree several times—they didn't seem to have much patience in waiting for their turn.

I smiled at all the bird traffic that always seemed heavier in the fall months. It was almost as if I was in a trance watching the birds go about their morning. It felt good to be in this quiet space and how often I didn't take time to just be in this sacred space with nature. How easy it is to look past this form of life as if it isn't important, I thought. But what I do believe is that our connection with nature and the animals is vital to our evolution.

The birds weren't worrying about where they had to be next or wondering what their purpose was. I found comfort in that. How could I learn to be like a bird or any other animal, for that matter? I wondered. Is it really that easy to just *be?* It would be something I'd continue to ponder.

As I continued to immerse myself in savoring the moments and being with the birds I heard an inner voice say, *Be free. Be open. Have fun. Listen. Splash. Hop. Sing.* Were the birds sending me a message or reflecting my inner awareness? I wondered.

The leaves on the birch trees in the neighbor's trees were softly blowing in the wind and their wind chimes ringing in the distance. I was in a state of meditation, getting lost in nature unfolding in the way it always has—and always will be—not forced or rushed. I wanted more than anything to stay in this tranquil place as more words floated through my mind—*calm, quiet, serene, breathe.*

As I allowed myself to follow this inner sacred sanctuary, Joie's sweet face popped into my consciousness. I could feel the energy of her very strongly. It was if she was right here beside me. Was she agreeing with the birds and their message to me? Was this a lesson in taking in more of what is right in front of me and to understand that I too can be like nature and allow my life to unfold in an organic way?

Yes, Joie, I said silently, *I want to know more.*

I don't know how long I actually sat there lost deep within myself as my feathered sparrow friends and Joie's spirit guided me through this divine meditation. But at some point I was ready to move on with my day. Having just taken in the healing medicine of nature had my soul feeling abundantly full.

To complete the circle of what seemed an elegantly orchestrated time, I grabbed my deck of Grace cards. I was eager to see what message showed up today.

Direction—look for clues. Grace will lead us to the exact events and experiences we need at precisely the right time.

As usual, I had to read the card several more times because I continued to be amazed at how the synchronicity of my thoughts always seemed to match the message from the cards.

I'd come to realize that more often than not the clues in our lives will not be some huge, flashing neon signs declaring what it is we need to hear at any given point. We can spend much time wishing for the answers to come more easily, but then we risk losing out on the message that is vital—the message that taking time to go within is the only way in which to really hear what it is our soul is trying to convey to us.

Clues come like whispers, and we often don't listen for them until something tragic causes us to stop dead in our tracks. It is then that we are often called to try and figure out what it is that matters most to us. Then we tend to question *everything.* We wonder what it was that we could have done differently. We promise to pay closer attention. At least this has certainly been my experience.

And while I knew I wanted to live in deeper awareness, I also knew I needed to be gentle and forgiving of myself when I didn't do so.

Continuing my quest of rumination and quietude, I was finally feeling better at learning to flow with it. The urge to have to *do* something was dissipating. In being with my thoughts, seeing them for what they really were, allowing them to be heard, I was able to gently sift through them. I began to see the value in allowing this open space in my life.

The heaviness I had felt, like a ton of bricks on my chest from grief and fear, began to lighten too. This new skin I was growing into was feeling like the right fit.

A shift was occurring also as I found myself wanting to embrace happiness again and let go of sorrow over the loss of Joie and what was once my sense of purpose in my work with Frankie. I wanted to move on and begin anew.

In many ways, I understood this as *my purpose* for this particular time in my life right now. This was essential as a way in which I needed to learn to be okay in this place of the unknown. This, in essence, was the *work* I was meant to be doing for now.

The Grace card I chose at random that day added to the wisdom that was now part of the foundation guiding me toward deeper meaning and understanding of my sense of self.

Support—expect help. A divine power more magnificent than anything else that exists on the planet is ready to support your every move.

As I read this, it triggered a memory of a conversation I'd had with Dawn. I remembered her mentioning that I should accept help from others—that I had given so much of myself the past few years with Frankie, Joie and Nikki. I recalled how kind and gentle her voice was. She encouraged me that perhaps now was the time for me to accept whatever help that may come my way during this time of self-reflection.

This memory, and Dawn's wise words of wisdom, brought a lump to my throat and hot tears to my eyes. It was hard for me to accept help. But I also recalled during my coaching time with Diane how she told me that asking for help is actually a sign of strength, not weakness. I'd never looked at it in that way, but now I was beginning to see the truth in her words.

Thinking about all I'd learned and how much I'd grown during those two and half months of coaching with Diane, I was even more excited to share with her some ideas I had been exploring.

After once again capturing this new insight in my journal, I set my pen aside and went for a walk. When I returned home something happened that had me in complete awe.

I was trying to print a receipt from an online purchase I had made. When I clicked the icon on my monitor to print, my printer acted up and wouldn't print. I unplugged it from the wall and plugged it back in. It sputtered for a moment and then the light was back on indicating systems were all set to go. I expected the copy of the receipt to come out. But instead, this is what it printed:

Grief is a doorway to your deepest self.

My heart began thumping hard in my chest. Staring at what came off my printer I was stunned, looking in disbelief at the words printed on the page. Where in the world did that come from?

I thought perhaps it could have come from something I'd put in the scanner of my printer so I opened the top of it. Inside I found a card from a deck of cards by Cheryl Richardson called *Self Care* and the quote about grief and on the other side it said, *release.*

The odd thing was that I didn't recall when I would have put that card in there to scan it. I had no recollection whatsoever. Chills ran down my spine. I smiled and took this as a sign from the universe. It was exactly what I needed to hear in that moment.

It resonated because I had realized a new space had opened within me the past few days. I was seeing more clearly that my grief for Joie was leading me to a new place within myself. While I didn't always realize I was thinking of her, I believed that my subconscious was putting the broken pieces of my heart back together again.

Instead of continuing to feel sad over her loss, I was now more in awe over how I was growing and evolving just for having had her in my life. And I wanted more than anything to honor her life and understand the lessons she brought to me while physically with me. Plus, the teachings she was now conveying to me in spiritual form.

I was fascinated at how the mind works if we can learn to observe it from a nonjudgmental place. I circled back to my earlier thoughts examining asking for help, recalling a woman I'd met the year at *The Artist's Way* workshop. I wasn't quite sure why, but I felt called to reach out to her.

Also quite interesting was that this was the same woman who I'd been curious about for many years. I'd often seen her about in our small village—at the post office, the local café or the library—and found her somehow mysterious. It was something in the way in which she carried herself and how she dressed that I would call eccentric and artistic. Her hair of salt and pepper, cut into a bob, was oftentimes pulled back in a comb to one side.

At the workshop I learned that her name was Marie. For some reason I was drawn to her, and my curiosity only grew as the twelve weeks of *The Artist's Way* progressed.

Spirit put her name in my head for a reason. It was my job to follow through, even though I wasn't quite sure why. I had her email address so I sent her a note asking if she would agree to meet me for coffee. I shared with her that I wanted to talk to her about some ideas I had that I was researching.

She graciously accepted my invitation and two mornings later we met at a local coffee shop.

Sitting in a booth across from Marie, I told her that I was on sabbatical because I needed to try and figure out what I wanted for my future. She listened patiently as I listed a dizzying amount of ideas that to one degree or another I was thinking of pursuing.

"I'm scared that I won't ever find that one thing again that will light up my soul the way my work with Frankie did," I admitted.

Marie nodded in agreement every now and then as I continued talking. When I finally stopped, she paused, took a sip of her coffee, and then ever so gently she said, "Just trust the process. Be grateful for this time you have to think things through. Try and listen with your heart and just be open to exploring without any attachments."

At first it wasn't what I wanted to hear. Everything inside of me tensed up. I took a deep breath and decided best to keep my mouth shut and keep listening. After all, I reminded myself, I did seek out Marie for advice.

"Not everything needs to be figured out right away. Let things evolve organically," she added.

There was that word again—organically. Dawn had said this very same thing when I adopted Joie and was struggling with wanting her to follow in Frankie's paw prints. I was also struggling with wanting to honor the need to slow down. Marie's words brought Dawn's advice back to the forefront.

As I listened to her, I was suddenly mad at myself. Why did I always think I had to have everything figured out right away? How often did I need to hear something before it actually sank in and grew roots to stabilize me? I was often frustrated with myself for what seemed to be a lack of patience.

It was as if Marie was reading my mind as all these thoughts swirled like a tornado. "We can't possibly figure everything out all the time. We aren't supposed to. That is how life works."

She was absolutely right. I knew this, but I also wanted to control the outcome. I was doing everything in my silly human power to figure out an answer *now*. All because, (and when I was truthful with myself) was so that I didn't have to feel uncomfortable with facing the unknown.

Marie said, "It could be years that you feel in this inbetween place before you figure out what is next. I've been in the very same place myself many times, but you have to trust that it is okay."

While it wasn't what I was expecting to hear, it was a relief to hear this advice. I sincerely appreciated her honesty. Having had so many of these feelings for the past few months, and really since retiring Frankie in 2012, having this safe outlet to express myself with Marie helped me to sift through them and see them for what they were. And more importantly, that what I was going through was quite normal.

What a gift it was to have talked with someone wiser and older than me. We agreed to meet again in a few months. And little did I know at the time, but our friendship would continue to blossom into one of my greatest treasures.

Driving home later that morning, I was in a very peaceful state of mind. It was a good place to be. I had reached out for help and I was supported. When I got to the house, I continued to let Spirit carry me by following the impulse to take Kylie for a walk.

We headed for a small wooded area near home, where we had been walking quite frequently lately. The quiet and stillness of the woods was grounding for me. I was also feeling a deeper connection with Kylie since Joie had passed. I sensed that she was enjoying the one-on-one time with me, too.

The sun was warm on my face and the slight wind blowing through my hair felt good, too. I felt light and free, as if I was floating on a cloud in the vast blue sky. Soft music played in my ears through my earbuds connected to my iPod as Kylie and I took our time shuffling along a gravel path. We eventually came to a set of wooden stairs at the beginning of the woods. There are different areas as you walk along the trail that you come upon these wooden steps, built by local boy scouts years before to help make the trek easier to navigate.

Looking up and around, I noticed that the trees were beginning to show more of the vibrant colors of fall. The sky was different shades of blue, as if someone had stroked it with a brush of watercolor. I was feeling in a place of deep gratefulness for my life and my sabbatical.

I had no place I needed to be. The only place I really needed to be was with my soul. The unknown was beginning to be something I could rest in without too much fear. I didn't feel as afraid anymore and was opening more to just paying attention without expectations.

There were some leaves that had already fallen to the ground as I took delight in hearing the crunch under my shoes and Kylie's paws. Without really a conscious thought, all of a sudden I heard myself say out loud, "Hello Soul! How are you?"

I was a bit startled that this came out of my mouth! But when I paid attention to my thoughts in a nonjudgmental way I realized I was accepting that one chapter in my life was now closed, and that was okay. Another chapter would begin when the time was right. For now, it was my work to continue to check in with my soul and learn to just live fully into the moment right at hand.

As I continued my meditative walk, Kylie sniffing just a few feet ahead of me, I recalled Nikki recently telling me that my sabbatical looked good on me.

If we can just stay out of our own way, our inner light will find its way back to us. It's our job to acknowledge this and allow the space for a new unfolding to take place. While I understood we can't always be in this inner place of peace, I hoped that my new awareness of holding space for myself when I needed it, would have me visiting this inward place of healing more often.

As I got lost in more of my thoughts, some words danced across my mind like a young ballerina swirling across the floor. *Stay awake. Pay attention. Look. See. Love. Reflect. Contemplate.* They twirled around me as if each word was tied to a ribbon with a tiny bird carrying each one in its beak. They were reminders of the work I needed to do no matter what stage of life I am in. This is part of why we are here—to be observers of this thing called life.

Taking in a deep breath, I inhaled the fresh, crisp, air around me. I soaked in this delicious feeling that was enveloping my soul and sinking deep into my being.

A song by Nora Jones was playing in my ears and the words, "You humble me, Lord," and "feels like home" vibrated throughout my body in resonance of exactly how I was feeling.

Oh, how we come to many crossroads in our lives! And if we are humble enough, we can see clearly that we are never truly in control or alone. Surrendering to this can help set us free.

While our free will gives us choices, we can veer off the path at times with our life feeling not like our own. But when we lose our way, we can come back to the center of who we truly are just by really seeing the beauty all around us. Resting within that space is so vital to what it takes to fill us up once again so that our inner light can come shining through again.

Deeper and deeper I let myself sink into these thoughts that if I was going to live in a more peaceful state of mind I had to acknowledge that the controlling part of me would undoubtedly show up now and then again. But I had to befriend and honor it, and then let it sail on by.

The next morning, I sat on the sofa with a cup of orange blossom tea and my journal resting in my lap. I closed my eyes and within moments I observed a soft, pastel pink light in my mind. I watched with curiosity as it slowly descended down my entire body and then finally reaching my toes.

Opening my eyes, I noticed sunbeams were dancing on the living room wall in front of me. I was feeling deeply content. Acknowledging the comfort I was receiving I said out loud, "Oh, how I love my home. Thank you."

Picking up my pen and opening the cover of my journal, I revisited the time I'd spent with Diane, pondering the many ideas and thoughts from my recent visit with her.

One piece of wisdom she offered that day really sank in. She encouraged me to not put a timeframe on anything. But rather allow whatever was to find me to do so in a natural way. To let it flow and follow what feels right.

It reminded me of my conversation with Marie. Yet again, Spirit was supporting me with all the right messages from my earth angels. All I needed to do was heed their insightful wisdom.

Diane, Dawn and Marie were all right! I had been trying to put a timeframe on everything. It really was yet another reminder of how often one can jump into something else just for the sake of doing so. How we tend to do this out of fear we won't be taken care of. How we try desperately to fill the empty space because it feels uncomfortable, instead of allowing ourselves to *feel* our way through.

Glancing at my tea cup, I'd realized I hadn't taken a moment to read the quote dangling from the end of the Yogi tea bag. I always looked at these quotes as messengers from the Universe also so it didn't surprise me that I read, "Trust creates space."

I took a deep breath and let the words fill me with hope that this time of open space was exactly where I was supposed to be.

Many thoughts crossed my mind this morning. One of which, oddly enough, was thinking about housewives of the 50s and 60s. A part of me felt like I wouldn't have minded being a stay at home gal. I've always loved my home, oftentimes telling others that I tend to be a homebody.

But I also knew how important it is for me to find something that fulfills my soul—something just for *me*. And this brought me back to the issue that I think has been an on and off struggle for women for many years and how to balance it all.

While I knew I'd eventually want to leave this concentrated space of quiet and solitude, I was concerned about how I would balance it all again when I put myself back out into the world. I didn't want to find myself in a place again where I felt off kilter like I did after Frankie and Joie passed away.

Then I reminded myself that perhaps there is no such thing as balance. We seem to put all this pressure on ourselves to achieve something that we have been conditioned to think we should have. And perhaps, just maybe, we can have it all, but just at different times of our lives and not all at once.

One thing I knew without a doubt is that I wanted the simple and meaningful life I'd worked hard to build, even though I was questioning how it would look going forward. But this new place of being felt rather like an adventure in itself, learning to trust the process and seeing where it would take me.

Before closing my journal for the day I recalled another suggestion from Diane. She recommended gathering articles, poems, photos and quotes that spoke to me. She encouraged me to pay attention to what they could potentially mean for a new direction. "Perhaps they could be clues," she said.

Excited about the idea, I set my journal aside and dug through the wicker chest in my writing cottage to see if I had a binder where I could gather everything. The idea really resonated. I thought of it as putting together a personal map of myself and what mattered most to me.

Thinking about this map, it triggered another thought I'd had—something I'd wanted to investigate but kept putting off. Lately I'd been experiencing some breast pain, though I did feel it was perhaps due to being peri-menopausal. But over the years I'd also come to believe that our emotions can play a big part in symptoms that manifest in our body. And this especially seemed to be true when we are in the midst of a challenge.

I went to my bookshelf and pulled down a book by Louise Hay titled, *Heal Your Body*. It's a list from A through Z of common symptoms and diseases that can be tied to our emotional state.

Turning to the page on breast pain it read, "A refusal to nourish the self. Putting everyone else first. Overmothering. Overprotecting, overbearing attitudes."

In one sense this was hard to read as I couldn't quite see myself in this statement. But when I looked at it objectively while being gentle with myself, it did make some sense. As I thought more about how it applied to me my mind flashed back to the year 2004 when my chocolate Lab, Cassie Jo was diagnosed with terminal cancer.

I then thought about how nine months later after Cassie Jo passed away when Frankie became paralyzed. It was an intense and trying time learning to adapt to life with a dog who couldn't walk. But as I learned to navigate in a new way with Frankie, my life revealed a purpose for me that I found to be quite joyful and my mission began to help bring positive awareness to disabled dogs like Frankie and dogs in wheelchairs. While it had many learning curves from writing, to publishing five books, and speaking in public, it was a time I experienced much fulfillment.

After Frankie passed and Joie came into my life, it was another intense year of mentoring Nikki as she contemplated a split from her husband and eventually moved in with John and me. We guided her through her divorce and provided a place of comfort as she worked on getting back on her feet again. Three months later Joie died and Nikki moved out two weeks later.

All of these pivotal moments flashed through my mind rapidly. For a moment it felt intensely heavy—as if bricks were bearing down on my chest. I saw for the first time with clarity how I had been going, going, going, and giving, giving, giving. I had never really slowed down to take time just for me. I never allowed myself room to catch my breath. Hot tears of recognition of everything I'd been feeling filled my eyes while at the same time they washed away all the heaviness I'd been dealing with.

I grabbed a tissue and wiped my eyes so I could read Louise Hay's suggestion for coping with breast pain. It said, "I am important. I count. I now care for and nourish myself with love and with joy. I allow others the freedom to be who they are. We are all safe and free."

There was no doubt in my mind I'd just been guided from Spirit and this was another step in a renewal of my sense of self.

Wisdom Found

The stirring up and close examination of the past ten years was helping to open new channels within my inner world. I reminded myself that there was no rush to fill it, but to just continue to follow impulses that felt right for me as I moved through the last few weeks of my sabbatical.

And acting upon this, I knew that today was the day I would visit the animals at Villa Loretto Ranch. Grabbing my journal and a pen, I hopped in my car and headed west. It was a beautiful day as the last days of September. The sun was shining high in the sky and the temperature was in the low 70s.

Driving down the highway I thought about the discussion I had with Dawn about hosting an animal communication workshop. She would be visiting Wisconsin from her home state of Alaska in the summer, and it felt like the perfect time, though I worried whether I could find eight to twelve people who'd want to participate.

As the doubt came in, I decided to change my thought pattern. Over the past month I'd often found myself talking out loud to myself, and I now said, "The right group of people will find their way to my animal communication workshop." I let it go out into the universe and knew if this was to be, it would happen.

Arriving at Villa Loretto Ranch, I parked and headed to the entrance. My neighbor, who works there as the Director of Food Services for the nursing home, knew I was coming. I had sent her a message on Facebook a few days earlier and she agreed to meet me when I arrived.

She walked me through the front hallway to the rear of the building. "Just go through that door and you will walk down a path right to where the animals are."

I thanked her and out the back door I went. Within a matter of minutes I was standing in the midst of several animals. They were everywhere I looked—straight ahead and to my left and right—and my heart immediately filled with peace.

I slowly walked down the winding gravel paths, taking in the animals along the way—first bunnies, then chickens and birds. I marveled at how quiet it was, but at the same time I could feel so much life vibrating around me. I felt like I had discovered this sacred place that seemed hidden from the world.

I took note of how it is that when I'm among animals I find myself in this inner center of serenity. I knew I wouldn't want to leave. But I took my time strolling among all the animals, basking in each special moment, and in awe of all the different creatures God created.

Except for the few volunteers, I was the only person ambling about that day. It felt like heaven on earth to me, as if I had my own private zoo, and all the animals were there just for me.

Realizing I still had my journal in my hand, I decided I didn't want to do any writing while here. I just wanted to *feel* into each precious moment with each animal I came in contact with. I wanted to just let them fill me with their wisdom. I found it so healing even though I couldn't find words to express how I was feeling. All I knew was that it felt like I was floating, while at the same time I felt very rooted in my being.

After a few hours of being among the animals, I drove home with my spirit feeling lighter and freer.

I still felt their effect the next morning as I found myself once again thinking of adopting another special needs dachshund. I really wanted my own little friend to care for and I silently said a small prayer that the right dog would find me once John and I returned from our trip to Asheville, North Carolina at the end of October.

The last day of September would be here in two days. It was time for me to make a decision if I was going to continue my sabbatical for another month. Though I felt I'd made a positive amount of progress, I also wasn't ready to immerse myself back into too much *doing*.

Since our vacation would take up half of October, I decided that taking the rest of this time to continue to marinate in quiet and unpressured possibilities. But one thing I *was* ready to do was expand on my writing, other than journaling just for me. I was feeling this inner nudge to sign up for a month long program by Writing Coach and Author, Cynthia Morris, called "Free Write Fling."

Writing in a different way, with daily prompts provided by Cynthia, and being within a group felt right. I would be held accountable being that we were encouraged to share our experience of writing daily in a private Facebook group. I knew this would help me to slowly ease back into my writing in a more public way. I was also curious to see what this might reveal to me by writing in this new approach, rather than just for myself.

While a part of me missed being active on Facebook, I had to admit I liked how rested and quiet my mind now felt. While social media has been such a valuable tool for me with meeting so many people I'd not have otherwise, at times, it had also zapped much of my energy.

Before I committed to another month of time for myself, I updated the readers of my blog. I told them know how much I missed them. I also shared with them my remarkable sign of the water paw print from Joie.

Lastly I told them three things I knew for sure after my thirty days of reflection:

1. I want to continue writing for my blog and newsletter. I want to continue writing about dogs and animals. I want to also continue to write about what a simple, authentic, joyful and meaningful life looks like for me.

2. I want to adopt another dachshund with IVDD. I'll begin my search when I return from vacation at the end of October.

3. I want to continue to be an advocate for dogs with IVDD and dogs in wheelchairs. I want to also continue to help guide others faced with this challenge with their own pets and give them hope.

After writing the post, I knew in my heart I'd be back at the end of October to commit fully to sharing my writing in public again. I felt a renewed sense of excitement and anticipation. It made my heart sing!

Resting into the final month of my sabbatical, I was definitely more in balance with my mind, body, and spirit. Following my strands of curiosity, like a spider weaving her web, this began to feel like a fun game—a game in which it was okay that no matter what impulse I followed it would serve as a stepping stone to the next phase of my life's journey.

After I published the post to my blog, I flipped through a journal of quotes I'd collected over the years. I oftentimes do this as a way of outside confirmation for what I'm feeling inwardly. A quote from Bernie Siegel's *The Art of Healing* leaped off the page.

*Loving and healing our lives is not only about dismantling
disease; it is also about being healthy, at peace, and fulfilled.*

As I pondered that thought for a moment it truly was
another testimony that taking breaks in our lives is essential to
our well-being. Somehow, someway, even if just for a day, an
hour, or five minutes—building these moments of stillness into
our daily lives has to be of importance. If we don't, we run the
risk of jeopardizing our health, living in an unsettled state of
mind—or both.

It felt especially empowering to have taken this leap of
faith, even though a month earlier it had felt incredibly scary.
While I still had moments of doubt, they were few and far
between now.

Later that day, I opened my email to find the most lovely
note from Lynne—a friend who is a healer and who had helped
me move past a block I had years before. I remember how
I was getting ready to write my first memoir but was having
a difficult time beginning. Through meditation and discussion
Lynne helped me reveal my fear. I was afraid that once my book
was complete, sharing all the years of my life with Frankie and
what she taught me, that it would mean the end of Frankie's
life and she would die. By giving voice to my fear I was able to
move on and write my book.

Lynne was aware that I'd been on sabbatical and having
been on them herself before, she understood very well this
inward journey I was on.

In her email she attached the most beautiful photo of the
sun filtering through the trees in her backyard.

She wrote: "I just left my desk because I saw this out my
window and went outside to stand under the light. This is for
both of us, as I was thinking of you and God showed up. I
knew I needed to stand under His light. As I did, I said, "Show

me what is next. I stand with you, I walk with you. You are in me, as I am you. All the while you were in my heart as well."

It took my breath away reading this from Lynne. She continued, "I then went into the woods and found two puff balls, which we eat. I am letting some things go too. It is the right time and my energy needs to rest. We have much work ahead of us and it is good to pause now."

There was that word again: *pause*. How often we dismiss its importance, as it seems to have no value in our culture. But there is so much innate wisdom in it, if we only stop long enough to observe and sit within its gift.

More clarity found me in that moment, that this was indeed Joie's gift to me—one of the reasons we were brought together by a big plan in the cosmos. She wasn't meant to be with me in physical form for too long; her teaching would prove way more valuable after her transition.

Had she not left her body, I'd have not awakened to living more into this essential awareness of how important reflection, refilling the well, and surrender is for my life to be more in balance.

As the days of October softly tumbled one into another, I became lighter in my step, deeper entrenched in Spirit, and even more grateful for the lessons bestowed upon me.

I also knew now with an even stronger conviction that when one door closes, another opens—that when we lose something we love, we truly never lose it, something will come to fill that ache in our heart once again. It also occurred to me that this is why we are ultimately here on this earthly plane—to continue to expand our hearts and our understanding of being human.

This is *the* purpose—to deepen our compassion, to walk in more conscious awareness, and to tune into our inner world for answers. By doing so, the wisdom one gains is that joy and peace only come from within.

Afterword

Your journey has molded you for the greater good, and it was exactly when it needed to be. Don't think that you've lost time. It took each and every situation you have encountered to bring you to the now. And now is right on time.

— ASHA TYSON

Every dog I've been blessed to love has marked a passage in my life. And if we look at our existence on this earth as a passage or a portal to the next realm, time does not matter, nor really exist. Though I can't say I always grasp this fully, I can say now that I understand it more—especially when I think of dear Joie.

She was here for me as it was meant to be. She arrived right on time and left on time. It was up to me to move inwardly to discover that transition in the form of her leaving her physical body, and my stepping into a time of reflection and slowing down, was a gift of another marked passage in my life.

On November 14, 2013 I adopted another dachshund with IVDD from *On My Way Home Rescue*. While she has disc disease she does not need a wheelchair to get around like Frankie and Joie did. And I also didn't break my promise this time (well, sort of). I waited until John and I returned from vacation, but I do have a confession to make.

It was two weeks before we left for Asheville, North Carolina that I discovered through a Google search an endearing, adorable doxie named Gidget. When I watched a video of her done by the rescue, I was immediately head-over-heels in love once again. Okay, so I can see you dear reader, grinning from ear to ear. You knew this would happen, now didn't you?

But this time, I handed it over to Spirit and silently said, *Okay, Spirit. If she is the one, I am trusting that when I return from my time away, she will still be available.*

I do have to say I was pretty proud of myself that I did well trusting in the process this time. I really didn't give Gidget too much thought while we explored the artistic and eclectic city of Asheville for ten days.

But it was on the second to last day of our vacation, having just finished breakfast in our red chalet part way up a mountain, that I could no longer contain my cautiously optimistic and guarded secret.

John was sitting at the kitchen table, perusing Facebook on my laptop. I said, "Can I show you something really adorable?"

"Sure."

I had bookmarked the video of Gidget so it was easy to access. Cue the music! *Wait 'Til You See My Gidget* by Johnny Tillotson. As the music played, across the screen flashed Gidget, a gray, black and tan dapple doxie being held in someone's arms. Her head is cocked to the side while also leaning back causing her ears to fly up over her head. Then you see her on someone's lap, stretched out on her back as if in a trance and in complete belly rub heaven. As the rest of the video plays you can't help but think that song by Tillotson was written just for her. She is tiny, quirky, and sweet. She is truly a Gidget!

I was relieved as the video finished playing to see that John was smiling. He looked at me and said, "So is she the one?"

"Well, I hope so. I kept my promise this time. I found this video of her right before we came here, but I've not yet contacted the rescue. I decided to wait and trust that if she is meant to be ours that she will still be available when we get back home."

And she was and she is a joy and Kylie wholeheartedly accepted yet another doxie into our home. Kylie continues to be my steady rock and the one who grounds me simply by being in her gentle, calming presence.

As winter approached I was happy to be snuggled on the couch in the evenings with the woodstove burning, my nose buried in a book and Miss Gidget snuggled at my side. I thought about how Joie's passing opened the door for Gidget to find her way to me. How my heart now was being given another chance to expand once again.

Though in the months ahead I'd still find myself struggling on and off with the question of "what's next" I took comfort in that I now had Gidget as my dear, new companion. And I reminded myself that everything else would work itself out.

While doing some volunteer work with a non-profit group that helps challenged young girls, I came across something that intrigued me. It was a 5 x 8 card with different images collaged on it sitting on a shelf. I turned to another volunteer, with whom I was helping to plan a retreat for the girls.

I picked it up and said, "What is this?"

"It's a SoulCollage® card," she said nonchalantly. She didn't offer any more information as we needed to finish the details of the retreat. But I was mesmerized by how the images on the card spoke to something deep in me, though I wasn't sure why. I was also fascinated by the word, Soul Collage, not realizing at the time that it is actually spelled as one word.

When I got home that evening I did a Google search and learned more on the website. In three days I read everything on SoulCollage.com and watched every video. I was enamored! SoulCollage® as stated on the website is, *a creative and satisfying collage process. You make your own deck of cards—each collage card representing one aspect of your personality or Soul. You use the cards intuitively to answer life's questions and participate in self-discovery.*

Unfortunately there weren't any workshops being offered in my area. But there was a weekend training to become a facilitator coming up in the fall at Holy Wisdom Monastery. I told myself I would give it more thought, but the truth was I couldn't get it out of my mind. I knew I wanted to take the training. Even if it was just for my own personal growth, I was being called to do this.

On a blustery, cold weekend in November 2015 I became a SoulCollage® facilitator. It was a deeply gratifying weekend, being with twenty-two other women from around the country.

I've facilitated some workshops to date and each time it has been a joyful, enriching, and rewarding experience. Gathering a circle of soul searching women together never fails to offer some thoughtful insight and unexpected nuggets of wisdom for everyone. Each gal seems to leave with a boost of empowerment and inspiration.

While some workshops I've taught online and plan to continue, I also now have a space in my home called Joyful Pause Studios. I welcome those wanting to know more about SoulCollage® and wanting to take time out of their busy lives to pause, reflect, and enjoy an easy, fun creative process.

In the spring of 2015 I was somewhat caught off guard with a phenomenon that exploded via the media and what they were dubbing, "She Sheds"—the idea being that if a man can have his "man cave" then a woman should be entitled to a space of her own, too.

While the term was new, the idea of a woman having a room of one's own wasn't new to me. Since 2009 I've had a ten by twelve space that my husband built for me that I've dubbed my "Zen Writing Cottage."

It is perched off the end of our deck and it's where I've spent countless hours writing, advocating for dogs in wheelchairs and dogs with IVDD, dreaming, working on new projects, evolving in my spirituality, practicing yoga, meditating, napping, reading, and visiting with dear friends.

Comments posted on Facebook from various articles being shared about this phenomenon varied from supportive to some that were quite derogatory. The negative, sarcastic comments bothered me, and though I understand they weren't directed at me personally, they sometimes felt hurtful.

I realized I had an opportunity to share a positive message about "She Sheds." And my message was to try and empower women to know that they deserved a place of their own where they can take time to pause from always taking care of others. And in my experience, it had enhanced my marriage.

Little did I know that a blog post I wrote titled, *How My She Shed Improved My Marriage* would ultimately land me on the websites of ABC, Today.com, and CBS, plus a satellite interview with *Weekend Sunrise* (Australia's number one breakfast show), and a variety of other blogs that would either pick up my post and share it, or interviewed me and wrote their own article.

But it was the TV interview done by CBS 58 out of Milwaukee, Wisconsin that I am the most proud. They truly captured the essence and value of what my writing cottage means and what a she shed can mean for women. They called the piece, *How My "She Shed" Helped Me Reach a Higher Calling.* You can watch it for yourself here:

https://youtu.be/7Hwsxv36keU

I still recall vividly how I came to a poignant realization as co-anchor of CBS 58, Marshanna Hester, and I stood on my deck after the interview, while Brian Urbanek, Videographer, took snippets of video inside my writing cottage.

I was staring at the front of my cottage, awash in complete gratitude for the opportunity that was unfolding that afternoon. It felt somewhat surreal. Marshanna picked up on the vibes I was likely exuding and said, "What are you thinking right now?"

Somewhat startled by the question, I replied, "Well, honestly, I'm feeling a lot of gratitude right now. But I'm also realizing what a gift transition really is. For the past three years, since losing my dachshunds, Frankie and Joie, I felt so lost. I didn't know what was next for me or how I could continue to make a positive difference in the world, which I had done with great gusto while Frankie was alive. After Joie died, I realized I had to listen to that inner voice that had been nudging me for a long time even though I found it difficult at the beginning of a sabbatical I took to slow down and value the gift of just learning to *be*."

She nodded as I continued. "But by allowing myself to accept being in transition, which in reality has lasted three years, has brought so many unexpected gifts. One being that I never would have thought I'd be standing here with you today talking about my writing cottage. This is truly a wonderful opportunity I've been given to encourage and inspire other women to follow their hearts. It's also a message I'm happy to be sharing that pausing more often in our lives to listen to our inner voice is something that our society needs to value more."

She nodded in agreement and two hours later it was a wrap. Brian and Marshanna headed back to Milwaukee to complete the editing of the interview which would air in July 2015.

A short story and photos of my writing cottage was also published in May 2016 in a book by Affirm Press titled, *She Sheds—A Treasure Trove of Women's Creative Spaces.* While I didn't realize the book wouldn't be available for purchase in the US (at least at this time) when I agreed to do it, I'm honored to have been a part of the project. I also realized another great opportunity, and am currently working on writing my own story of how my writing cottage came to be, to be published in the near future. Stay tuned!

As I look back over the last three years, I understand more fully that transition will come again—it is inevitable. There are times in our lives where we will have major transitions such as losing a loved one, a pet, retirement, children leaving home, a major illness, or losing a job, just to name a few. But I've come to an awareness that we really are in transition every day of our lives, which often happens on a smaller scale.

For example, finishing the writing of this book, I will now transition to getting it out into the world, or each time I learn something new or change my perception of something, I make a transition. We are in transition as the sun rises, then sets, and as each season changes. We are also in transition as we age. It's not something we can escape, but something we must embrace at each stage.

Like challenges, which Frankie taught me to find a blessing in each one, Joie has taught me that transition has blessings to bestow upon us, too. And if I can find the courage to embrace each passage, moving through them with an open mind and heart, my life will be enriched with the gift of wisdom and grace…and it is wisdom and grace that invites joy and peace to take a welcome seat at the center of my soul while here on this earthly plane… and that which will ultimately walk me home.

A Note to the Reader

If you would like to see Joie rolling in her wheelchair
we have a video for you online:
https://youtu.be/y7KMe1JNMYY

Resources

- EDDIE'S WHEELS: designs and manufactures custom dog wheelchairs and wheelchairs for a variety of handicapped pets, eddieswheels.com
- DODGERSLIST: organization dedicated to providing education, resources, and help to those whose pets have been diagnosed with Intervertebral Disc Disease, dodgerslist.com
- THE FRANKIE WHEELCHAIR FUND: grants wheelchairs to disabled dogs in need. Donations always welcome, nationalwalknrolldogday.com/donate-to-the-frankie-wheelchair-fund
- NATIONAL WALK 'N ROLL DOG DAY: honoring and celebrating dogs in wheelchairs who teach us to embrace each day with love, hope and joy. Founded in 2012 and celebrated every September 22, nationalwalknrolldogday.com and on Facebook/ National Walk 'N Roll Dog Day
- ANIMAL COMMUNICATION: Dawn Baumann Brunke, animalvoices.net

Acknowledgements

I must first thank my dear, sweet, Dachshund, Joie. For had you not entered my life, though our time together was so short, the gift you left behind is deeply meaningful to me. The wisdom you imparted now resides in an inner sacred space of my heart and continues to be my guide in choosing to find joy in all the simple pleasures of life.

To my loving husband, John. Not only for enduring the ups and downs of a writer's life, but for opening your heart once again to love another special needs dog...well, make that two more since we now have Gidget. Thank you for always supporting my heart.

To my mom, for your continued belief in me, and for always popping your buttons. Your love and support of me gives me the courage to expand my wings a little more every day.

A grateful thank you to my friend and animal communicator, Dawn Brunke, for your gift of understanding the animals. I'm very grateful for the messages from Joie that not only helped me better understand her needs, but guided me to opening my awareness to what it was I needed to understand to grow and evolve into a better human being.

To Dan Blank for helping me see through your caring and dedicated work as a mentor helping creatives, that being in transition is part of the journey. But most of all for your gentle reassurance that my taking a sabbatical was the right thing to do.

For that once in a lifetime opportunity, thank you to producer Jeff Gendelman and director Gil Cates, Jr. for choosing Joie to play a part in your movie, *The Surface*.

A heartfelt thank you to Linda Klein for all her help, and getting on a plane to fly my new bundle of joy to me that would be my Joie. I'm forever grateful.

To my editor, Dana Micheli, for helping me bring my voice to the page once again.

To graphic designer, Caryn Newton for capturing what I envisioned for the cover of this book and for your attention to detail in guiding me to bringing my book to production.

To my family and friends for your encouragement in big and small ways. I'm grateful.

Last, but not least, my faithful followers whether we connect on Facebook, Instagram or my blog, your enthusiasm for my writing is such a gift to me.

About the Author

Barbara Techel is the author of *Through Frankie's Eyes,* her first memoir, and two children's nonfiction books, *Frankie the Walk 'N Roll Dog* and *Frankie the Walk 'N Roll Therapy Dog Visits Libby's House.*

Since 2007 Barbara has been advocating for dogs with Intervertebral Disc Disease (IVDD) and for dogs in wheelchairs. In August 2012, after the passing of her first wheelie dog, Frankie, she founded National Walk 'N Roll Dog Day and established The Frankie Wheelchair Fund. To date, the Frankie fund has granted over 55 wheelchairs to paralyzed dogs in need through the generous donations of others. Frankie's legacy also lives on through a special spot dedicated to her at a book garden for children in Sheboygan, Wisconsin called Bookworm Gardens.

Barbara's journey with Frankie, and then Joie, has been featured in numerous books, articles and blogs. As well as, the special space where she writes called her Zen writing cottage, which has been featured on the websites of ABC, Today.com, and CBS.

When not writing, Barbara enjoys encouraging women to tune into the whispers in their hearts, practicing yoga and meditation, reading, date nights with her husband, and spending time snuggling with her two dogs, Kylie and Gidget.

- To connect with Barbara visit her website, joyfulpaws.com.

Find her active on these social media avenues:
- Facebook.com/joyfulpaws
- Instagram/barbtechel
- E-mail: barb@joyfulpaws.com